THE
MONEY
CONFUSION

THE
MONEY
CONFUSION

How Illiteracy About Currencies and

Inflation Sets the Stage for the

Crypto Revolution

JOHN TAMNY

All Seasons Press
2881 E. Oakland Park Blvd. Suite 456
Fort Lauderdale, FL 33306

Interior design by Kim Hall
FIRST EDITION: OCTOBER 2022
Library of Congress Cataloging-in-Publication Data has been applied for.
ISBNs: 978-1-958682-26-5 (hardcover), 978-1-958682-25-8 (ebook)

9   10   7   8   5   6   3   4   1   2

To Ed Crane, from whom I've learned so much, and who most crucially taught me how to think.

ACKNOWLEDGEMENTS

I'll begin with the person to whom this book is dedicated. I went to work for Ed Crane and the Cato Institute nearly twenty years ago as a fundraiser. This has been the ultimate education as Cato's supporters are a source of endless knowledge which has had a profound impact on my thinking. In this role I got to know Ed, and our friendship has grown ever since. We didn't always agree about money and inflation, but I came to see how correct he is that freedom logically precedes any policy discussion, including any discussion of money. In teaching me how to think, Ed brought me to this book's foremost point about money: it is a natural market phenomenon the quantity of which we never need to concern ourselves with. That Ed agrees with this book's foremost point means more to me than he'll ever know.

Jeff Yass is one of the many remarkable people I know. Particularly in 2021 and 2022, Jeff was a major source of confidence. Somehow while running a global financial behemoth, Jeff found the time to read some of my opinion pieces and letters-to-the-editor making a case that "rising prices" had little to do with inflation. Better yet, he took the time to compliment my analysis with which so few people agreed.

Bob Reingold has generously agreed to meet with me several times a year for many years. Our visits have been very useful not just because he's such a great friend, but because he has always brought so much business knowledge to our discussions of public policy. As my wife would readily confirm, I reference Bob's maxims with great frequency, and plan to mine his great mind for many more in the years to come.

Hall McAdams has patiently discussed money and inflation with me since October of 2003, when I first made his acquaintance in his cavernous Little Rock office. I came to discuss Cato, but the conversation quickly turned to money and inflation. It continues to this day. Hall is very accomplished in business, and retains an active quest for knowledge, which he has sometimes pursued with me. Since 2003 Hall has made himself available to answer my many questions and has responded to the countless ideas I've bounced off of him. Without Hall, I never would have had the courage to write a book so counter to the conventional wisdom about inflation.

I also met Richard Masson through the Cato Institute. It was 2005, and he generously took time out to talk about the Institute. The discussion migrated to money and inflation, which Richard knows well for many reasons, including his status as one of the world's foremost collectors of currencies from all eras. Richard's support has been particularly meaningful in 2022 given the growing divide on the matter of inflation. Richard's unwillingness to join the herd as it redefined inflation altogether has meant a great deal to me.

Joan Carter is the former President of the Philadelphia Fed, but she has always treated me as a colleague, as has her husband, John Aglialoro. John's career began auspiciously on Wall Street, after which he and Joan together achieved remarkable entrepreneurial success. They have both cheered on my work. Joan is also Chairman of FreedomWorks, where I work. What a great boss!

Adam Brandon is President of FreedomWorks, and since 2017 has given me the freedom to write without restraint. I'm beyond grateful, and as I always tell him, he's the best organization head in Washington. Which means he can't leave FreedomWorks without taking me with him. This is true even if the Cleveland Browns secure his services. If he doesn't know it yet, we're a package deal.

Kristina Crane is Ed's wife. She has been an energetic leader and shaper of the libertarian movement almost as long as Ed. Kristina now manages the FreedomWorks office but does so much more. It is a joy to work with her and learn from her.

Noah Wall and Spencer Chretien work tirelessly on the various programs that give FreedomWorks life. What they do makes it possible for me to share my ideas on freedom with millions of activists around the country. Kim Drezdon puts up with me, and as my wife will attest, that fact makes for a much better home life.

John McIntyre runs RealClearMedia, where I'm an editor. John has given me freedom for many years to write in contrarian fashion, and to combine a wide range of opinions on matters involving economics and markets. This freedom is what makes RealClearMarkets the ultimate source of opinion and news.

Kim Dennis (and the Searle Freedom Trust that she heads) has been a highly generous patron of my work for years. Over fifteen years ago, and without knowing me, Kim allowed me use of an office at Searle, and from there a friendship bloomed. She knows how grateful I am for getting to do the work that I do, which the Trust helps make possible. Kim's colleagues Richard Tren and Courtney Myers similarly rate special mention for supporting me all this time.

It's hard to talk about joy and work without bringing up George Will. At lunch back in 2015, George told me how excited he is to get back to the office and write. What he said has stuck with me ever since. Being able to write is a *privilege*, and something I can't wait to do each day.

If George Gilder was the individual most quoted by Ronald Reagan, he's now the individual most quoted by me. Downward mobility some would say. I've learned so much from him over the years, which means it's a major thrill to have him endorsing my book, and better yet that he agrees that "too much money" is what happens *after* the inflation.

Steve Forbes and Nathan Lewis remain lonely voices out there preaching sanity on the matter of money. So few say, as they do with regularity; that money is a *measure*. That Steve remains the nicest person I know just adds to the thrill of working with him in pursuit of sound money.

Right up there in terms of kindness is Ken Fisher. With every e-mail he sends there's always a question about my family, my own well-being, and my thoughts. Ken could so easily be remote, but he's the exact opposite. I learn so much from, which makes me very fortunate to know him. Ken's been an inflation skeptic amid a mad rush among economists and pundits to define rising prices. Ken's own skepticism gave me confidence.

So did Bill Walton's. An energetic critics of the lockdowns from day one, it was only natural that an investment banker and highly numerate thinker like Bill would question the conventional wisdom about inflation. When so few were willing to tie the errant lockdowns to downstream horrors including fractured production processes, Bill was. And with his eponymous show, he gave the contrarian voices a platform from which to offer opposing points of view.

Bob Landry and I have been talking money and monetary policy for years. In 2021 and 2022, Bob and I not only talked it as is our routine, but did so with growing alarm about the worrisome straying on money and inflation from people who've agreed with us in the past. Bob is one of the very, very few who sees money as a natural market measure, and I'm very grateful to have him as an ally in 2022, and well beyond.

Rob Smith is one of the best—and funniest—writers I know, and someone who gets all this stuff intuitively. His writing on the price impact of the horrid and unnecessary lockdowns related to the coronavirus very much informs my chapter in the book about the inflation that quite simply wasn't. He has articulated over and over again in his *Real-ClearMarkets* columns that higher prices born of the evisceration of supply chains were an obvious consequence of the lockdowns, but crucially had little to do with inflation.

Richard Rahn, Jeff Erber, Scott Barbee, and Dan Mitchell are part of a weekly lunch group that Ed Crane leads, and that I don't miss. That they won't agree with some or a lot (Rahn) that's in this book speaks well of them, and hopefully the book. It's the disagreement with conventional wisdom that gives *The Money Confusion* life, including with Rahn who has cheerfully taken the opposite side on the inflation question. All that, plus he may agree more than he realizes. Richard has long made the point (and witnessed up close) how good money invariably pushes out the bad, which is a major theme of this book. We may join hands still.

Rafe Resendes has so generously and graciously backed me for so long. So has the whole Applied Finance team, including Daniel Obrycki, Saul Marquez, Chris Austin, Maggie Resendes, and Paul Blinn. These are all financial savants who, despite knowing so much more than I do about markets, have always given me a stage from which to voice my opinions.

In the past year, I've begun doing work related to technology and antitrust with Charlie Sauer and Norm Singleton of The Market Institute. What principled, clear-thinking individuals they are. At a time when partisanship has warped so much commentary, they continue to call balls and strikes on both sides. It's a treat working with them and learning from them.

My parents, Peter and Nancy Tamny, continue to support what I do. Not only did they watch me grow up, but they observed my fascination with money over the years and the evolution of my thinking. My contrarian nature had to come from them, which is one of many reasons I'm so grateful to them. My sister Kim is so good to me, and much more important, is so good to Claire and Reed. As always, I don't deserve her and her kindness.

Claire and Reed (a.k.a. "Wiggles) are the kids, 6 and 2 respectively. They bring so much joy and purpose to what is called "work." It all speaks to a beautiful future for the kids. I expect to be awed seeing the career paths that Claire and Reed will someday choose. As much fun as they are now, I can't wait to enjoy their future.

All of which brings me to my wife and mother-to-the-kids-extraordinaire, Kendall. Thank you so much for all the inspiration, and sometimes much-needed tough love. None of this would be possible without you, and I hope you know how grateful I am. You regularly tell me that the money stuff is "so obvious," and you're right. The problem is that monetary experts don't feel as you do. Hopefully what's common sense to you eventually becomes common knowledge.

TABLE OF CONTENTS

INTRODUCTION

"The sole use of money is to circulate consumable goods." – Adam Smith, *The Wealth of Nations*

Desperation in the air, carnage in the streets, money lit on fire. Choose your cliché. The main point is that the presumed future of money seemed anything but in the summer of 2022. According to the pundit class, cryptocurrencies were a past tense concept—but we're getting ahead of ourselves.

For now, it's useful to note that the monetary future was instigated by endemically poor government oversight of traditional paper currencies. Yet the spark that lit the crypto flame was, in some ways, immaterial. What matters is that the flame was lit, enabling copious amounts of investment to follow. That so much wealth had been wiped away in this digital gold rush is very much a statement of the obvious: change has never been easy. Failure, and lots of it, is an essential ingredient to success. The wealth lost on aggressive speculations in crypto is a sign of a much smarter sector, and one poised to create a very different tomorrow. Good, trusted money is an essential driver of progress, and the mis-named "crypto bubble" has us on the path to much sounder money and a better future overall.

At risk of trafficking in cliché, the summer of 2022 was a time of blood in the newly paved cryptocurrency streets. As prices broke to lows not seen in years, and decentralized lenders faced mass liquidations, even those most bullish on the "future of money" started to reconsider. One-time billionaire investor Mike Novogratz, one of the more prominent crypto bulls given his impressive wealth, summed it up in a no-nonsense way: "This has been a complete and total old-school ass-beating."

The former partner of Fortress Investment Group left his "TradFi" firm in 2015 to pursue the unbound promise of crypto and quickly became its leading voice. But by summer of 2022, there was little reason to cheer.[1] After reaching an all-time high of $68,000 in November of 2021, Bitcoin, the sector's realistic pioneer, was down to just a shade above $19,000. "Crypto winter" once again hit the headlines and everyone from teenagers on TikTok to "experts" in financial media proudly declared crypto dead once and for all.

The majority believed that the "crypto bubble" had popped, and that little was left for the newest popular delusion. In fact, a Google search for "crypto bubble" in June of 2022 unearthed over 51 million results. Though it was, and still is, the easy conclusion to make, it remains thoroughly flawed. "Bubble" is the catch-all word for every market crack-up. Implicit in its silly notion is that there exist markets populated by buyers only. During the "bubble," buyers throw money at anything they hope will increase in value, with little regard for risk. Amid surging markets for crypto in which so-called "Fear of Missing Out" (FOMO) took over, it's understandable that those observing from a distance could have this perspective.

Of course, such a view is utter nonsense. In any market there are, by definition, buyers *and* sellers. There's no mechanism for a buyer to express his or her "FOMO" absent a willing seller. Perhaps even more crucially, for a feverish crypto believer to express his deep belief in the marketplace, a crypto skeptic must be allowed to express an equal amount of pessimism. Put another way, markets are defined by the passions of the bulls, the bears, and everyone in between. And for those who believe the passion of the buyers overwhelmed the uncertainty of sellers, this too fails basic scrutiny. Such a view would imply that sellers were unaware of the FOMO qualities of buyers, but logic dictates otherwise. Participants may vary, but markets in aggregate are wise.

If 2022 wasn't a popped "bubble", then what was it? After all, the carnage was real. Hundreds of billions of dollars' worth of savings were destroyed. If not a speculative mania driven by wild-eyed visions of immense crypto wealth, then what? What some would call a "bubble" was, in truth, a positive sign of *economic progress*. We need many more of what the lazy in thought errantly describe as "bubbles" and it's easy to see why.

The answer, among others, lies in the arrival of Novogratz to the proverbial crypto gold rush. As readers know, he wasn't the only arrival. At which point we need only ask a basic question: would Novogratz have pivoted in this direction absent surging crypto prices and the profits that could be had from markets that at times seemed to only go up? The answer is no chance. What some indolently described as a "bubble" was in fact the crucial migration of essential, information-producing capital to the crypto space. Call the manic prices the lure for investment without which an alternative-currency future would be much less likely. Courageous savings shape the future. History will say they did in 2022, and as they did 175 years before.

175 years ago, most people had a good sense of what they would be when they grew up. In fact, most knew their profession before they even had a chance *to* grow up. Since the technologies that could compound the work of one man were still largely in the future, most knew they would spend their lives on farms. With eating a necessity, but the creation of food an uncertain endeavor, life was spent surviving. The way out of subsistence living was through the productive use of excess output—what economists today refer to as "savings". When the productive are able to *not* consume or spend some of the fruits of their labor, they can put that gathered wealth to work as investment. Simply stated, savings are what make a new and better future possible.

Absent the investor excitement that pushes previously unknown concepts to new heights, there would be very little investment. Without investment, stasis reveals its ugly self. The common dictionary definition of stasis is "a period or state of inactivity or equilibrium." Today always resembles tomorrow in societies defined by a lack of investment; it's a cruel life.

Though crypto reminds many of the still widely misunderstood "Tulip mania" and other speculative crashes, its role is much greater than a footnote in financial history. To see why, it's essential to travel back in time—not quite so far as "pre-pandemic," but to 2021. It was then that a nascent cryptocurrency sector was in the throes of immense popularity. "NFTs" had become a household term and debates over new concepts of art and ownership came into the fold. It was an era defined by change, with even the most traditional of cultures encountering something new. We're of course referring to a particular troop of Japanese monkeys, but don't give up on the storyline just yet.

To understand ourselves and our path ahead, it pays to keep an open mind.

In 2021, Yakei, a nine-year old Japanese macaque, took control. Commonly referred to as "snow monkeys," this "highly intelligent species" is native to Japan and "well known for its beet-red bottom and affinity for soaking in hot springs" according to *New York Times* science reporter Annie Roth.[2]

Yakei was rather unusual in that she "[presided] over a troop of 677 monkeys in Takasakiyama Natural Zoological

Garden." While females are the leaders among bees, hyenas and elephants, Roth reports that females at the top of the monkey heap are very rare. Her ascendancy was no small feat either—"by violently overthrowing the alpha male of her troop," she became the first "female leader in the reserve's 70-year history." Yakei didn't just knock the alpha male off his lofty perch that brings with it all manner of perks, including better access to "food, mates and resting locations." She defied the "strict hierarchy" within macaque troops that places females below their mothers in addition to the males. Clearly, Yakei was uninterested in tradition; but more interestingly, she had an almost Machiavellian willingness to rise. She "beat up her own mother to take the top spot among females of her troop" before ultimately taking out the alpha male.

Reserve employees at the Zoological Garden witnessing the events decided to test if she truly had become the proverbial "top dog". How did they confirm Yakei's status? Laying out peanuts for the macaques, they anxiously waited to see who would stand at the front of the line. The results were undeniable, as "[males] and females stepped aside to let Yakei eat first."[3] The macaque experience speaks to a universal truth among species of all stripes, including humans. Life is about the *getting*. *Getting* is how we survive. For a primate species, *getting* is plainly a violent, zero-sum act. The unequal, like Yakei, eat more and better because others eat less and worse.

All of which requires a pivot. From the Zoological Garden we have a vision of how animals operate, and it's kind of horrifying: violence ultimately pays the bills. Contrast that with life in the shimmering United Arab Emirates city of Dubai. Within this desert metropolis stands the world's tallest building, the Burj Khalifa. The superlatives attached to "the Burj" are many. In addition to its half-mile into the sky stature, the Burj can claim the world's highest nightclub on the 143rd floor, and the world's highest observation deck on the 148th.[4] To say that the Burj, or "tower" in English, is a remarkable human achievement is quite the understatement. That humans could erect something so remarkable speaks to our distinction from animals. The ability of humans to work together or "trade" is at the core of what makes us so productive. When they divide up work, and exchange value for value, humanity can quite literally create structures that pierce the sky.

It's useful to recall certain lessons from the eighteenth century in thinking about the Burj. A myth persists to this day that with the writing of *The Wealth of Nations*, Adam Smith essentially invented capitalism. The legend confirms that Smith's unrelentingly brilliant book is sadly one of the most well-known but *unread* books in the world. Smith invented nothing, nor did he pretend to. As *Wall Street Journal* deputy editorial page editor Matthew Hennessey explained in his 2022 book *Visible Hand*, Smith didn't invent capitalism as much as he "wrote the plain truth about how humans live, work, play, and interact with each other."[5] Smith was *reporting* on the capitalist economy that he saw, and he was awed.

In the book's opening pages, Smith took readers to a pin factory. He crucially noted that one employee working alone within the factory could maybe—*maybe*—produce one pin per day. But several individuals working together could produce *tens of thousands*. With numerous brilliant observations about human action, there's an easy case to make that Smith's reporting on the specialized production within the factory was among the most important the world has ever known. It vivified the basic truth that work divided is the path to individual specialization, staggering productivity advances, and, by extension, prices that are always falling.

The reporting signaled that while animals fight each other over a fixed pie of wealth, humans work together to *create* wealth. Wealth creation is a consequence of individuals doing the work most associated with their unique skills and aptitudes. It's worth taking a moment to reflect on the story of progress told in just these few words. As opposed to animals that can only use violence or theft to increase their shares of a fixed pool of resources, humans get to do what they do best with others doing what they do best in pursuit of what can only grow. We're rewarded for doing what most compliments our skills—the productive extensions of a rational mind.

All this tells a bigger story about the genius of open trade and the free exchange of value. Often, the focus centers on lower prices for goods and services, which is reasonable. When individuals around the world compete to meet our needs, the *getting* becomes increasingly abundant. However, the greatest attribute of the *getting* comes with ever-greater division of production. The more specialization increases, the more our own output reflects our most brilliant and bespoke individual traits. At a personal level, we understand this well. While doing work that has little to do with our specialties, the work is defined by little more than watching the clock. Conversely, when we're doing what reinforces us and allows us to express what we're best at, we frequently find ourselves irritable while *not* working.

All of which requires a return to the Burj. Though it's located in Dubai, architect Stefan Al described its construction as "Roman engineering, American rebar, and a German pump—all in the Arabian Desert."[6] What Al writes is crucial. Just as a pencil is the end result of global cooperation among countless producers, imagine the amount of integration of unique skills that goes into erecting a building that soars half a mile into the sky. Al is clear that the Burj is "an accumulation of inventions from all over the world," but the more important truth that is that absent know-how and production taking place among specialized individuals the world over, the Burj would not be standing.

Consider the ever-improving concrete that supports the structural integrity of these "supertalls." The fact that concrete keeps improving means buildings can grow ever taller. Absent it, buildings would collapse before completion since the doubling of a structure's height occurs in concert with an *eight-times* increase in its weight.[7] The operative question is how great minds have improved concrete. If one man would struggle even in the twenty-first century to make a pin if left alone all day, how is it that we have this remarkable material? Al confirms that the latter is a "product of human imagination,"[8] but more crucially it's "become quite the sophisticated blend."[9] The "blend" is the story here. Concrete that will transform the shape of cities and the way we live combines genius inputs from the world over—and that's just the beginning.

Though the concrete discussed here can withstand staggering amounts of weight, it's no simple task to transport it thousands of feet into the sky without it hardening prematurely. Enter German industrial giant BASF. Al reports that BASF has created "an admixture called Glenium Sky 504, a superplasticizer that keeps the mix soft for a full three hours upon arrival."[10] Problem solved? Not so fast. How do you transport the concrete in the first place? Had construction involved "hauling stones skyward," the building of the Burj would have been prohibitively expensive and, in turn, impossible. Another German corporation, Putzmeister, provides the answer. Specifically for the Burj, Al writes that "the company created the Putzmeister BSA 14000 SHP-D" that facilitated the quick movement of liquid concrete to where it was needed.[11] Taking nothing away from the brilliant business minds working in Dubai, it was truly the world's combined genius that made this remarkable skyscraper concept real. Odds are it will only get better. As global production becomes more and more interconnected, the ambition of production will stagger for its grandiosity.

Considering buildings alone, we're talking about structures that will eventually measure over a mile in height and encompass streets, parks, ski mountains, and all manner of other living-standard enhancers that are unimaginable but wholly possible the more that humans work "alongside" one another, even if working thousands of miles away from each other; that's just human ingenuity.

Imagine what happens if (and when) "robots" reach their expected potential. We already know from the days of Adam Smith how productivity soars when a few specialized individuals work together. Imagine what we can accomplish when human ingenuity is paired with billions and trillions of automated hands working twenty-four hours a day for 365 days a year. What's ahead is impossible to contemplate; there's no limit to what humans can accomplish when they're producing alongside billions and trillions of specialized people and automated facsimiles of the same. To think about it is to desire a longer life just to witness the accomplishments; limited only by human ingenuity, the extension of life could be one of them.

That the future for humans is bright calls for further contemplation of Yakei and her fellow snow monkeys. For them, the wealth pie is fixed. Access to food, mates and quality resting spots is directly related to strength, brute force and *getting* more such that others get less. How different this is from the human experience. Though wealth inequality has been perverted by economists, politicians, and pundits as a zero-sum notion—the human version of the brutality that defines life in the Takasakiyama Natural Zoological Garden—the reality is quite different. Stated simply, the *getting* among humans is about producing in abundance to get in abundance. The *getting* is what happens after we've produced value for others.

Why was the late Steve Jobs so rich? Among other things, he mass-produced a supercomputer that fits in our pockets. Elon Musk has redefined the very notion of the automobile into an ever-improving computer on wheels. Jeff Bezos made it possible for us to access the world's plenty with one click. While animals batter one another to get, humans succeed at *getting* by virtue of creating value for themselves and others.

Why the big difference between animals and humans? It would insult the intelligence of every reader to talk about intelligence disparities, so it won't happen here. It's better to present the finer point: humans create wealth and attain it to the extent that they're free to divide work with others. The freedom to work alongside others is an essential driver of immense progress. To the extent that we're free to work together and exchange the fruits of our labor, we progress. It does not insult the citizens of Dubai to say that the Burj could not have been constructed if the city were an autarkic island of economic activity. It doesn't take a village as much as it takes the world to produce everything from the pencil to the airplane to buildings so tall that temperature and weather are markedly different at the top than the bottom.

Why can we work so productively together? Money is a big factor—arguably the largest. Money is an agreement about value among producers that facilitates the division of labor without which progress would slow in brutal fashion. Though governments are, in a sense, monopoly issuers of it today, money was decidedly *not* an original creation of governments or central banks or presidents; rather money was the logical consequence of production. Reduced to the basics, the baker wants the vintner's wine, but the vintner has no interest in the baker's bread. He'd prefer the butcher's meat. As an agreement about value among producers, money makes it possible for producers with disparate wants to exchange value with each other.

When we work, we're working for money. But what we're really working for are the goods and services for which money can be exchanged. That is why a national mint or central bank or Treasury is realistically a *non sequitur* when it comes to so-called "money supply," "money in circulation," or most laughably, "money velocity." If you're talking about any of the three in your desire to understand money, it's safe to say your mind is wandering, likely down a path littered with misunderstanding. Realistically, no productive individual or business need ever worry about how much or how little money is circulating. Money is the obvious *consequence* of production. It's a natural market function instigated by production such that money is always where it needs to be in amount and quality. To see why, think again about what distinguishes humans, in particular prosperous ones.

Prosperous humans are servants first and foremost. They're rich precisely because they've discovered a way to profitably meet the needs of others. They will get what they want by producing for others. But barter is obviously inefficient and somewhat impossible since what we want to get is as varied as production in a market economy. There must be an agreed upon measure among producers that facilitates the exchange of production, and just as markets form naturally on the way to needs being met and discovered by producers, so logically did market actors produce money in several forms (cowrie shells, cigarettes, banknotes, IOUs, paper, etc.) to exchange things with one another.

It all gives life to the Adam Smith quote that begins this introductory chapter. Mid-paragraph, in a section of the book about money, Smith observed that "The sole use of money is to circulate consumable goods." What's funny about what Smith wrote with the present top of mind, is that that the passage wasn't underlined or italicized, nor did it end with an exclamation point. As mentioned, this most crucial of observations, one that is realistically the basis for this book, didn't even begin the paragraph. It was inserted in the middle, seemingly as an afterthought. The view here, hundreds of years later, is that Smith properly felt he was stating the obvious—when stating the obvious, there's no need for emphasis. ***On its own, money has no purpose.*** The latter will be emphasized in *The Money Confusion* simply because the nature of money has been so thoroughly perverted in modern times.

A measure of value conceived to facilitate the movement of goods and services possessing actual value, money has taken on mystical meaning to which it cannot measure up. What moves wealth is increasingly seen as wealth on its own such that thinkers (credentialed and otherwise) spend endless amounts of time contemplating "money supply," M1, M2, M3, velocity, too much money, too little money, and all sorts of misplaced thought. Their intensity about the supply of what is a natural consequence of production reveals their confusion.

Money isn't wealth on its own. It can't be eaten or planted in the ground on the way to more of it, but its acceptance among producers makes it possible for producers to exchange with one another and further specialize in the process. Money facilitates wealth creation because money is the logical consequence of production that facilitates more of itself. Since there's obvious benefit to be gained from easy exchange among the productive, there's obvious economic benefit to be had for those who finance the production and exchange of the same. This requires us to stress, yet again, the simple truth that no reasonable person would ever worry about the amount of "money" circulating in a city, state, or country. Money *has always* and *will always* find production simply because life is about the *getting*. When we produce a good or a service, we're aiming to attain equal value for it, at which point money that's viewed as a credibly stable measure of value will be circulated by profit-motivated financiers as a way of aiding the productive in their pursuit of value for their output.

It's all a way of stressing what some will mistakenly read as jingoistic, or revivalist, or as some weak attempt at an inspirational speech, but *we are the wealth*. We increasingly specialized humans, working side-by-side with humans the world over, are the wealth. Money is the measure or agreement about value, or the common language that makes our remarkable division of labor possible. If the measure of value is broadly agreed upon, the work done to create value or wealth is much more likely to take place. It's an odd paradox: money isn't itself wealth, but it's everywhere that wealth is being produced and exchanged simply because "the buyer of a thing is the seller of that which he gives in exchange."[12] The man who uttered these words, nineteenth century French political economist Leon Walras, got it.

The problem today is that few others do. And you as the reader will know this the moment that "money supply" and other alleged measures of wealth are discussed as though there can be too much or too little of what measures the value of production. Such a view is wrongheaded. It cannot be stated frequently enough that wealth is what specialized humans *create* in ever greater amounts the more they work together. And just as governments, monetary authorities and economists can't plan economic activity, they similarly can't plan or supply the proper amount of "money" necessary to facilitate economic activity. The obnoxious conceit is in the trying—it's wasted effort. What producers need is an agreed upon measure, or a reasonably agreed upon measure. After which, supply of the measure is ultimately production-determined. Where there's production, "money" to circulate its movement will arrive as if directed by, in the words of Smith, an "invisible hand." Where production is slight, so too will be money in circulation.

How much money should circulate? Such a question misunderstands the nature of money. Given the unlimited potential of humans to create wealth, the only limit to "supply" is the ability of humans to produce. In other words, there's no upper limit to money, nor a money floor if people find their ability to produce suffocated. Money is just the quiet measure that moves the fruits of our production around. Money is the most basic of concepts, though it's one that has long been hijacked by economists, politicians, and pundits in pursuit of the job security that comes from complicating that which isn't. The aim of *The Money Confusion* is to simplify what should be blindingly clear, in the hope that future discussions of what is a logical consequence of production won't be so ridiculous and confused. This will be done free of charts and equations, and realistically free of any requirements of pre-existing knowledge.

Indeed, if you the reader are willing to commit to memory the Adam Smith quote that opens this introduction, you're well on your way to understanding money's simple brilliance. As a facilitator of exchange, money enables the cooperation among the humans without which there is no economic growth. That's all there is to it.

CHAPTER ONE

THE MEANING OF MONEY

"Money does not pay for anything, never has, never will.
It is an economic axiom as old as the hills that goods and
services can be paid for only with goods and services."
– Albert Jay Nock, *Memoirs of a Superfluous Man*

It was 1992. Then-*Wall Street Journal* columnist David Asman was in St. Petersburg covering the rebirth of freedom in the former Soviet Union. He described the scene well, giving attention to the natural beauties of the Russian landscape beyond the city's once imperial streets. With the Iron Curtain lifted, a different ethos had begun to spread among the Russian people. They were, for the first time in a very long time, *free*.

Consider this through the lens of the lockdowns that politicians tragically pivoted toward in 2020 in response to a virus. Americans handled them well in a sense, but they could reasonably endure what was senseless because they had endless television, movies, food deliveries, exercise and so much else at home. Just as important, they were free to criticize what was a mindless seizing of freedom. Conversely, the Russians of the Soviet era had very few rights and little ability to speak out against the repression they suffered. Communism is about desperation; they suffered the suffocation of their spirit amid a state of material nothingness. Imagine their joy upon the dissolution of the Soviet state. Funnily enough, even the weather seemed to mirror the rebirth Asman was witnessing.

In one of his *Journal* columns, he wrote of how "It's a magnificent time for a magnificent city—a city with natural and manmade beauties that have acted as an ironic backdrop to some of the most beastly violence of the century." It was uplifting and profoundly sad all at once. Imagine having to *celebrate* the right to be oneself and produce for oneself. Production in the former Soviet Union cared little for the benefits of specialization. Labor was forced without regard or reward for skill, and it showed. With work a requirement rather than a natural evolution of free people blending their talents, the results were not impressive. Just as the Burj couldn't have been created by Emiratis in Dubai alone, neither could much of market worth be produced by Russians who were toiling within the literal boundaries of the state and the figurative (but very real) ones born of work divided among the very few.

Asman didn't just notice the beauty and joy that could be found in what had formerly been bleak. He also noted the joy of the workers. Increasingly, their work became reflections of unique, individual talents. He recounted the street performers "In the shadow of the Winter Palace" showcasing their skills for those walking by. "Russians rarely clap to show appreciation at these shows," he noted, but the performers didn't "much seem to care, concentrating instead on the ruble notes dropped in their hats by passersby." Where Asman's column became super interesting, at least for our purposes, was in his observation of the unique response to the sight of a U.S. dollar. Asman wrote that a "dollar causes an immediate halt to the performance while the performers thank the donor."[13] There are so many truths in what Asman wrote about the reaction of street performers to a dollar, but the most important is what it signals about money.

As the introductory chapter stressed, money is an agreement about value. While ruble notes dropped into their hats didn't elicit much of a reaction, dollars most certainly did. It raises an obvious question: why the big difference? The answer lies in the Albert Jay Nock quote that begins this chapter. Goods and services can only be paid for with goods and services. St. Petersburg's street performers were offering a service of sorts, and they stopped to thank those who dropped dollars in their hats because dollars could be exchanged for commensurate goods and services, quite unlike rubles. Asman's brilliant anecdote speaks to the truth about trade and money's role in it. We produce goods and services to get the goods and services we want. No one works for money; they work for what money can become.

In receiving the occasional dollar for their entertainment, St. Petersburg's newly free buskers knew they could *get* with dollars because the merchants they paid in dollars could similarly purchase real market items with this trusted money. It happily speaks to how credible money binds us and elevates us in enabling exchange of equal value. Money's role as an agreement about value allows us to specialize and, even better, circulates without limits where people are specializing. If we all did the same thing, it's safe to say we'd be miserable and there would be very little money circulating. Money is a happy consequence of individuals producing endless variety and exchanging it with one another, but it's also true that credible money wouldn't circulate in abundance where people aren't specializing via divided labor. It all results in remarkable achievements like the Burj. Think of the myriad advances that took place around the world before something as grandiose as the Burj could be built. Without feverish exchange among the specialized that is facilitated by credible money, remarkable creations like the Burj would be wholly imaginary.

This necessitates a discussion of monetary devaluation. While its presumed causes (real and imagined) will be discussed in later chapters, it's useful to consider devaluation itself.

It's sadly accepted wisdom among economists and their enablers in the media that shrinking the exchangeable value of currencies has a positive impact on economic growth. As business journalist Christopher Leonard observed in his 2022 book *The Lords of Easy Money*, "Devaluing the dollar wasn't seen as all bad inside the Federal Open Market Committee (FOMC). It made American products cheaper overseas, which could stimulate exports and create jobs."[14] Books could quite literally be written ridiculing the two sentences in quotes, but for now consider them a useful insight into what's believed inside one of the world's biggest employers of economists (the Federal Reserve), and what those economists convey to the business press.

An "economy" isn't some abstract blob. An economy is *people*. People in the U.S. earn dollars, but as readers now understand, they really earn the goods and services for which those dollars can be exchanged. This clarifies that devaluations harm the only "economy" there is—people. To be clear, this isn't some call for the poor and middle unable to hedge against money mischief to get out their pitchforks. The view of this author is that easily the biggest drivers of prosperity and staggering living standard advances are the super-rich. Currency devaluation robs workers of all stripes, the super-rich most economically cripplingly. We all work for money to get things and devaluation means we get fewer things.

It also means production becomes more expensive in terms of the money we're using; that or the money is no longer useful altogether. To see why, consider once again the street performer in St. Petersburg or the contractor in Dubai. The goal for any work product is to exchange output for goods or services of equal value. If the dollar is devalued, it's only reasonable that those transacting in dollars will gradually require more of them for the same amount of goods and services. When you think about it, that is a statement of the obvious. Consider all of this in terms of what Leonard wrote about the Fed's view of devaluation allegedly making products "cheaper overseas." Every market good in the world is a blend of specialized production around the world. No doubt there are "American," "Chinese," and "Japanese" exports, but what precedes the finished good is cooperation well outside the "country" allegedly exporting the good. Consider Apple's iPhone. As UC Berkeley professor Enrico Moretti explained it in his 2012 book *The New Geography of Jobs*, "If you buy an iPhone online, it is shipped directly to you from Shenzhen [China]. Incredibly, when it reaches the American consumer, only one American worker has physically touched the final product: the UPS delivery guy."[15] The iPhone is designed in Cupertino, CA, but is created around the world. Hillary Clinton was incorrect about it taking "a village." The miracle of modern production (and pre-modern production too) has workers at all points on the global map at work. *It takes a world.*

The Burj is a miracle, but it is also a miracle that we carry supercomputers around in our pockets which are available for lower and lower prices. These miraculous prices are the logical fruits of cooperation among workers rewarded for the efficiency of their production. An iPhone solely produced with American inputs either wouldn't exist, or if it did exist, would be both expensive and somewhat rare. Thinking of all this in terms of money, the real nature of currency devaluation becomes clear: short of a willingness among workers the world over to provide U.S. producers with output in return for a fixed amount of dollars worth ever less in terms of real goods and services, currency devaluation must take place alongside rising costs to reflect the currency's shrinking value. There's no competitive advantage to speak of despite what's believed at the Fed, inside the U.S. Treasury, and inside newsrooms. And the story, or the meaning of money, doesn't end there.

A few paragraphs prior it was said that "easily the biggest drivers of prosperity and staggering living standard advances are the super-rich." The rich, by virtue of having copious amounts of unspent wealth, can put what's unspent to work in pursuit of the creation of products, services, and inputs that enable the creation of ever more products and services. In contemplating this, please think about the myriad global inputs that go into the creation of the iPhone, or perhaps better yet, think about BASF's Glenium Sky 504 superplasticizer that delays the hardening of concrete, or the Putzmeister BSA 14000 SHP-D that pumps the liquid concrete ever higher into the sky. These advances didn't just happen. They were the results of voluminous experimentation that often ended in failure. It's useful to point out that the very excellent industrial lubricant WD-40 only achieved on-the-market-shelves quality after forty tries. This was the Rocket Chemical Company's sole product.[16] Imagine that—forty tries for WD-40. How many tries before Glenium Sky 504 proved useful? How much money was spent on its development?

All of which speaks to how essential the extraordinarily rich are to progress. Since they uniquely have money to lose on the most outlandish of ideas (and yes, a pump meant to transport liquid concrete thousands of feet in the air was, at least at one time, outlandish), they're the drivers of progress. Reflect on this in terms of currency devaluation. When investors put wealth to work, they're doing so in pursuit of returns in money that can be exchanged for other things. Never forget, life is all about the *getting*. Repeat it over and over again that no one buys and sells with money, pays or is paid with money, lends or borrows with money, or buys or sells shares with or for money. Underlying every monetary transaction is access to the goods and services for which that money can be exchanged. When the rich invest, they're delaying consumption of goods and services now on a hunch that they'll enjoy monetary returns that enable much greater access to resources down the line. Hopefully this clarifies why currency devaluation lays such a wet blanket on progress. Why put wealth at risk now for uncertain future returns denominated in dollars exchangeable for much less than those ventured? Call devaluation a tax on saving.

This helps explain why economists are such fans of currency devaluation. They near monolithically believe that consumption is what powers economic growth. Under this model, devaluation is grand—if dollars will be worth less one, five, and ten years from now, the obvious choice is to consume with abandon now rather than pursue devalued returns in the future. Of course, as the above description should make clear, consumption is not what powers growth. Consumption is the consequence of growth that is logically a result of savings. Savings are what make possible intrepid leaps of entrepreneurs and businesses to rush a much better future into the present. Jobs spring from investment, as does the pursuit of new products and services. It's those advances achieved by billions of increasingly specialized workers around the world that lead to supercomputers in pockets and buildings that pierce the sky.

Still, it must be stressed that all this progress springs from a global division of labor that becomes more and more sophisticated with each passing day. Money is the lubricant of this division, and in particular credible money that enables relentless exchange among individuals attaining products and services for products and services. Debase money, as in devalue it or destabilize it, and you slow the natural division of work so crucial to progress while also slowing the investment in advances that will enable ever greater specialization among individuals.

CHAPTER TWO

THE MEANING OF STABLE MONEY

*"The Individualistic Capitalism of today, precisely because it entrusts saving to the individual investor and production to the individual employer, **presumes** a stable measuring-rod of value, and cannot be efficient— perhaps cannot survive—without one."*
– John Maynard Keynes, *A Tract on Monetary Reform*

Words are never equal to war. When it comes to describing the suffering and devastation war entails, words don't do the job. The use of "indescribable" almost certainly achieved lift-off from vain attempts to recount the horrors of war, but it's left to more inquisitive readers to scour the internet for exact details of timing and geography.

Germany after World War II merits the claim of indescribable devastation—yet authors try. In his excellent 2021 book, *Aftermath: Life in the Fallout of the Third Reich, 1945-1955*, German journalist Harald Jahner did his best to provide readers with a sense of what little remained in the country. Among other "indescribables," Jahner reported that "The war had left about 500 million cubic metres of rubble behind," which if piled up, "would have produced a mountain 4,000 metres high."[17] That's over 12,000 feet. With the Burj looming in the background as an example of what happens when humans work together instead of killing one another, the combined pile of rubble in Germany would have amounted to roughly *four* Burj Khalifas.

All of which requires a brief digression, but a necessary one for a book aiming to discuss money in a reality-based way. Recall from the previous chapter that economists claim currency devaluation is a source of economic acceleration. It's amazing even the ignorant could believe something so at odds with the human cooperation at the core of immense progress. Somehow in their higher learning, or more likely *before* graduate programs confirmed the beliefs they brought to campus, economists concluded that shrinkage of the money measure we earn enhances progress and prosperity. Notable about economists is that it's not just on the subject of monetary devaluation that there are overwhelming majority beliefs. It's also broadly accepted by the credentialed that the maiming,

killing, and wealth destruction that was World War II lifted
the U.S. economy out of the Great Depression. It would be
difficult to find a more horrifying and *sicker* viewpoint than
this one, but it's nevertheless the view of most economists.

The simple truth is that *people,* yet again, are the economy,
and war *exterminates* them. Nothing could be more of a
growth deterrent than war simply because war rubs out the
very people who divide up work on the way to productivity.
Having dug a big hole of massive contradictions in claiming
an upside to government spending on armaments to destroy
humans and wealth, some hedge with a bit of nuance. What
economists really mean, apparently, is that with much of the
post-war world destroyed, the U.S. economy thrived because
U.S. workers and corporations had very little competition.

For readers of this book, hopefully the Burj, Apple's
iPhone, and the globalized production of all finished goods
race to your minds the next time you read or hear about the
alleged economic upside of the Second World War. There
was none to be had, nor was there economic upside for the
U.S. once the war ended and our corporations were largely
alone atop the world stage. War by its very name shrinks the
global division of labor so essential to progress, which means
there are no economic winners; rather, there are only degrees
of substantial loss. This digression is required as a way of
reminding readers of the reasoning that guides economists.

All of which brings us back to post-war Germany. Even
in the worst of times, amid mass devastation, people still
pursue goods and services. Arguably the *getting* becomes even

more urgent, for obvious reasons. In the case of Germany, the people were starving. Amid the starvation, the government intervened (as governments do) to offer "ration cards" to the populace. The cards allotted 1,550 calories per day to each German,[18] an amount woefully insufficient for health, let alone prosperity. Worse, given that governments can't decree anything into existence, there was little effect in the way of food supply. As such, ration cards didn't always command 1,550 calories, and the result was the formation of real markets outside those born of command from high places. As Jahner so pithily puts it, "Any market restriction automatically creates its own black market."[19] The ration cards were so useless against the on-the-ground reality that "the illegitimate economy was threatening to devour the legitimate one."[20] In other words, markets always assert themselves. No doubt some markets are quieter than others, and certainly less vibrant, but the fact that life is about the *getting* means that real markets will form amid the chaos of government rations and other price controls.

Money invariably finds its way into the marketplace as people need a means to expand exchange beyond simple barter. What's crucial about Germany's post-war desperation is that governmental monetary authorities were hardly the source of the money that was liquefying the real economy. Extra crucial is that the money economy formed will help answer the question that some readers have been asking since the Introduction: what does he mean about money being a consequence? Why is money a certainty? Doesn't some monetary authority have to create it for circulation? In short, no—money is abundant where there are goods to be exchanged, and scarce where there's little of market worth.

This is important because the official German currency was no longer dependable as a measure of value. There loomed the possibility of currency reform that would have rendered the circulating Reichsmark invalid as legal tender. Though such a reform sounds weighty, it wasn't truly a problem, in a sense. Jahner writes that "cigarettes took the place of banknotes. The cigarette became the cowry shell of the post-war era. *Its exchange rate might have fluctuated, but it remained one of the more dependable certainties of those years*" (author's emphasis).[21]

Imagine this for a moment. What is money but an agreement about value? Regarding the exchange of goods and services, it's only logical that money as a measure of value would be *dependable*. At least reasonably dependable, otherwise trade would revert to literal barter. Few producers are going to produce real market goods for money that may not be accepted by other producers, or that if accepted, would exchange for quite a bit less owing to unstable value. The cigarette had a fixity of value that the Reichsmark didn't, for it to replace the official currency in markets that mattered. Think about this in terms of excitement about the dollar in post-Soviet Russia versus a ho-hum nod of the head to a ruble. In the words of John Maynard Keynes, "Money is important only for what it will procure."[22] And in Germany, cigarettes procured all manner of items unrelated to smoking, including sex. As Giles Milton reports in his 2021 book about a wrecked post-war Berlin, *Checkmate in Berlin*, "A night with a German girl cost five cigarettes." Milton adds that twenty-five packs of cigarettes could be exchanged for a "state-of-the-art Leica camera."[23] Milton confirms Jahner's reporting about the reliability of Germany's official, government-sanctioned currency versus cigarettes circulating in much greater volume. In his words, cigarettes were Berlin's "most sought-after currency, because they were far more valuable than the debased mark."[24] Just as markets for goods and services ultimately assert themselves amid the chaos inevitably created by government interventionists, so do markets for currencies form.

All of what's discussed here will be revisited in later chapters, but for now it's useful as a reminder of what was confidently stated in the Introduction about how the productive needn't worry about too little money in circulation. For fun, let's say that *precisely because* economists worry about the quantity of money in circulation on the way to calls for government planning of the same, serious people should not. Even in rubble-strewn countries like post-war Germany, measures of stability emerge such that the little market worth remaining in existence can circulate; markets always speak. That markets speak requires more thought about money itself. As the Keynes quote that begins this chapter makes plain, capitalism *presumes* a stable measuring rod of value. We know this because wherever goods are traded, it's inevitable that the medium most known for stability as a measure of value emerges as the unit that referees most exchange. It's a shame something so obvious must be stated, but this book will be full of such statements. Underlying the assertion that producers require money that is stable in order to transact is the logical desire among producers to get goods and services roughly equal to those they produce. Again, obvious stuff.

From what's obvious, it shouldn't surprise anyone that money's evolution was about a search for something stable as a definer. Eventually gold emerged as the definer of money not based on religion or mystic sunspots or because it shimmered, but because in the words of nineteenth century political economist John Stuart Mill, it's the commodity "least influenced by any of the causes which produce fluctuations of value."[25] For money to be most useful, it needs to be quiet, or "low-entropy" to quote the great modern polymath, George Gilder. Money is only necessary as a way for producers of actual wealth to trade, but what a necessary input it is! If its value is stable, there's one less deterrent to trade among individuals and there's one less deterrent to savings and investment. Stable money as a measure of value doesn't ensure that every trade will yield better or equal to what was produced, nor does it ensure that every investment will yield positive returns—but it does ensure that we won't lose value for using money to buy, sell, lend, borrow, or buy and sell shares.

To see why, consider Bitcoin. Imagine being asked to remodel a friend's bathroom with a payment plan of one Bitcoin now, one in six months, and one in twelve months upon completion of the job. Is it unreasonable to suggest that any proposal of the kind mentioned would elicit a subsequent ask of "which Bitcoin?" Would it be the one exchangeable for $68,000 in November of 2021, the one fetching roughly $19,000 in June of 2022, or perhaps the one that sold for $2,500 in July of 2017? Bitcoin's fluctuations speak to its weakness as a currency as this is being written. Put more bluntly, it's not money right now due to its wild instability. That Bitcoin is talked about so animatedly is the surest sign of it not existing as real money. Real money is quiet—its value doesn't change. Is the foot, pound, or minute even discussed outside ways to measure other things? In the words of Mill once again, "As it is much easier to compare different lengths by expressing them in a common language of feet and inches, so is it much easier to compare values by a common language of pounds, shillings, and pence." Currencies were eventually measured in terms of gold for the same reason that we measure height, weight, and speed in terms of feet, pounds, and minutes. Gold has a constant quality to it much like the foot, pound, and minute. It is perfectly stable? No, but it's as close as market actors have come to stability, which explains its use as a definer of money values across time. To be clear, gold ascended to the top of the money heap via *market forces*, not central planner decrees.

Hopefully readers can see why gold became money— the most *money* of money is that which is stable. Gold once again isn't as constant as the foot, pound, or minute, but it's the commodity that attained the most constancy as a stable measure. What verifies the previous assertion is the well-known truth that gold emerged as money around the world over the centuries and it remained the definer of world currencies right until the early 1970s.

The last gold standard prevailed from 1944 until 1971. At the Mount Washington Hotel in Bretton Woods, New Hampshire, monetary authorities from around the world got together to recenter the global monetary system around the gold standard with the U.S. dollar in a key supporting role. The dollar would be convertible to gold at a fixed rate of $35 an ounce while the other participating nations would peg their currencies to the dollar, thus achieving currency stability. From the standpoint of stability, the regime was a success; for workers and capital owners alike, it was a highly effective monetary system.

How can readers be more certain of the "stability" offered by the above-described gold standard? To be fair, skepticism is warranted. Arguably some of the worst publicists for gold as a definer of money are its most ardent advocates. "Gold bugs" make all manner of claims about the Federal Reserve, the Rockefellers in cahoots with central banks, Wall Street, so-called "money supply pumped into the economy," and so on. The sad truth is that the vast majority of gold advocates haven't the faintest idea as to why it's so useful as a definer of money. The good news is that there's no need to rely on the confused certitude of the cranks. Instead, we can look to Craig Karmin, a longtime editor at the *Wall Street Journal* who has never caucused with the gold standard crowd. Let's refer to

Karmin as a conventional thinker about money, which means he broadly supports the PhD standard that prevails whereby dollar policy is *planned* by monetary authorities as opposed to gold's price stability being used to *define* the dollar.

In 2008, Karmin published *Biography of the Dollar*. It's a very useful book for its revelation of how much the dollar, even in its present floating state, referees transactions the world over. This notion will achieve more airtime in later chapters. What requires mention here is Karmin's casual observation that up until 1971, there "was no need for a foreign exchange market because all major currencies were pegged to a dollar rate and could only be changed in unusual circumstances."[26] Yes, you read that right. Before the dollar's explicit gold link was severed in the early seventies, there "was no need for a foreign exchange market." When you think about it, it makes perfect sense. If Adam Smith were alive today, he'd marvel at the very notion of currency markets. If you doubt this, consider the Smith quote that begins this book: "the sole use of money is to circulate consumable goods."

Implicit in Smith's illumination of the obvious was that money just *is*, much like the foot, pound, and minute. Money is the quiet measure around which prices are formed. In the words of Gilder, money "is the central information utility of the world economy."[27] Money, in a normal world, is the stable measure that acts as a price giver for everything else. To Smith, trading currencies would be like trading feet, pounds, and minutes—wasted effort. The markets seemed to think the same about money when it had gold as part of the definition. Indeed, as Karmin clarifies through his history of the dollar, there was no need for a foreign exchange market when the dollar was pegged to gold simply because there was nothing to trade. Currencies were serving their purpose as quiet measures. Evidence supporting this claim was the lack of markets for currency trading.

Where it gets interesting is in the events that followed. As we know, Karmin was writing about what prevailed before President Nixon's decision to sever the dollar's link to gold. What happened after? As of the publication of Karmin's book in 2008, the currency market was the "biggest market in the world, with a daily trading volume of $3.2 trillion."[28] When Gilder's *The Scandal of Money* was published eight years later, daily currency trading in the world's biggest market had soared to $5.3 trillion.[29] It's not in published form yet, but Gilder has subsequently relayed to the author that that $5.3 trillion figure has doubled as of 2022 to somewhere north of $10 trillion, which is very telling. What it reveals is that money defined in terms of gold provided a substantial benefit to global commerce. Evidence supporting this is the frenzied daily trading of currencies that never took place before money was detached from the yellow metal that made it *money*. Losing status as a reliable measure, the billions and realistically trillions worth of global trade in goods that takes place every day must occur alongside trading of the measures themselves.

Why the trading? Think back to the Bitcoin example in this chapter. Though contracts are still denominated in dollars, pounds, euros, yen, Swiss francs, and very few other currencies, the currency number placed on those contracts is no longer trustworthy. Since money's value is a floating concept where it used to be a stable one, contracts and other forms of trade denominated in money must be hedged based on the unreliability of money itself.

Why was it "obvious" that money measured in gold "provided a substantial benefit to global commerce," as argued above? Money is most useful when its value is constant and gold imbued money with constancy. Producers of actual goods and services *chose* gold as money par excellence many centuries ago, and we can clearly see why ever since politicians cheered on by economists left the "auto-pilot" stability that gold provided. Trading in currencies has soared. The markets have spoken again. With money no longer as reliable without its golden anchor, trading in currencies has gone skyward as market-based evidence of this truth. Money was deprived of what made it *money*.

Where it becomes interesting, but not surprising, is that economists cheered this move. We can among others return to Christopher Leonard's *The Lords of Easy Money*. A book shaped by the views of economists, Leonard wrote that if "the gold standard worked, people would still be using it."[30] Except that they *are* still using it, as evidenced by the frenzied currency trading that has emerged after gold's explicit link to money was severed. While monetary authorities in the employ of government can be wrong with great regularity, and even use being wrong to gain more funding for whatever it is they claim to work on, failure in the real world brings with it a pink slip either slowly or all at once. With money no longer reliable as a measure in the way that it was before 1971, currency trading has surged as a way of mitigating the chaos wrought by unstable money. $10 trillion in daily currency trading is evidence of just how well the gold standard worked—but this truth is something most economists have little interest in considering. You see, economists generally look askance at the gold standard or commodity-defined money. Gilder has cited a 2012 bipartisan poll of economists conducted by the University of Chicago in which 57 percent "strongly disagreed" with the gold standard.[31] Daily currency trading in the years since 1971 indicate that actual market actors don't share economists' disdain for money that is stable as a measure. Given some of the deeply held beliefs of members of the profession, we shouldn't be surprised by their scorn. If anything, we should take their fear of replacing PhDs or the "PhD Standard" with the gold standard as the surest sign of the utility of the latter. Money once again exists to facilitate the movement of production, which means money is most useful when its value is certain—basic stuff. In short, the economists have it wrong.

And they're not just incorrect about floating money values versus true money, defined by stability. They're also incorrect in their belief that money defined in commodity terms somehow restrains its supply. This falsehood, including the laughable notion that a gold-defined dollar caused the Great Depression, will be addressed in the next chapter.

CHAPTER THREE

MONEY FINDS YOU

"What he really lends is so much capital; the money is the mere instrument of transfer. But the capital usually passes from the lender to the receiver through the means either of money, or of an order to receive money, and at any rate it is in money that the capital is computed and estimated."
– John Stuart Mill, *Principles of Political Economy*

"I expect really long hours until we succeed, and you're going to be asked to do the impossible."[32] Those were the words of Elon Musk to engineer Scott Alexander. It was 1999, and Musk had just directed $12.5 million of his $21.5 million in proceeds from the sale of Zip2 to his new financial start-up, X.com. Canada's Queens University was Musk's first North

American stop after leaving his native South Africa. While in Canada, Musk interned at Bank of Nova Scotia. According to biographer Ashlee Vance, while there, Musk "had an inkling that the bankers were doing finance all wrong and that he could run the business better than anyone else."[33] Paradoxically, Musk learned a lot while learning very little during his time at one of Canada's foremost banks. X.com would be his response to "how lame banks are."[34]

Except that changing what's "lame" is never easy. As Jimmy Soni reported in his 2022 book *The Founders*, a history of PayPal, Musk was taking on a seemingly insurmountable challenge in his efforts to innovate around banks. It's hard to imagine now, but at the time of X.com's founding "only 10 percent of all online commerce was conducted digitally—the vast majority of transactions still ended with the buyer sending a check by mail."[35] Yet Musk imagined a world of rapid payments, banking, and investing all online. So, in a sense, did Peter Thiel and Max Levchin, founders of Confinity Inc., the company that X.com would eventually merge with to become PayPal. Yet there was little demand for what the non-conformists envisioned, and as for banks, they were typically lagging on the vision front. As a J.P. Morgan Chase executive haughtily explained to a Confinity consultant, "We just don't see people being comfortable getting away from cash, ATMs at the time, and credit cards."[36]

Change is hard, which explains why most startups in Silicon Valley fail. Eager to rush an all-new future into the present, they can only do so insofar as they're able to change the minds of consumers perhaps understandably set in their ways. With money, multiply that challenge. What could be more frightening than moving one's savings from a sturdy, well-secured, *physical* bank to an online one? When Musk said he was asking recruits to do the impossible, it was an admonition about a near-term future that he saw all-too-clearly. The odds of success were exceedingly slim, and evidence supporting this claim can be found in PayPal's market capitalization today: that it's worth $98 billion as of this writing is clear market evidence that essentially no one felt the vision of Musk, Levchin and Thiel to move payments online had a chance of succeeding. Though there's ongoing debate about "efficient markets," there's no debate about whether $100B opportunities are passed on by the commercially established. PayPal's worth today is the surest sign of how very much the dominant commercial players of the time thought Musk et al. were nuts.

And so began what Soni described as "a four-year odyssey of near-failure followed by near-failure."[37] In Musk's own words to Soni, PayPal "was a hard company to keep alive."[38] The startup faced the prospect of running out of money with some regularity, only to secure new investors seemingly at the last minute; including the closing of a $100 million funding round in 2000. PayPal veteran Mark Woolway contends in counterfactual fashion that "If the team hadn't closed that one hundred million, there would be no SpaceX, no LinkedIn, and no Tesla."[39] That's how close PayPal came to closing its doors.

It's said that a week in politics is an eternity, and it should be said that a day in finance is something more. The world can change in an instant. Think back to March of 2020. In the previous month, U.S. stock markets had hit an all-time high due to optimism about the future, yet by the midpoint of March, streets around the world were increasingly empty as a result of lockdowns related to the coronavirus. Crashing stocks reflected surprise about how quickly panicky politicians had done so much damage.

Much changed between 2000 and 2001 in technology. While the Nasdaq reached all-time highs in March of 2000, by the following year stocks (and technology stocks in particular) were enduring a sickening decline. Whereas the Internet was all the rage in the first year of the twenty-first century, by the second it had become a punchline. Think about this in terms of PayPal's funding prospects. Particularly in the U.S. amid so many technology failures, the adventurous nature of investors was at a low ebb. A company that was hard to keep alive during the best of times faced the ugly prospect of sourcing continued funding during difficult times, and particularly brutal ones for businesses with ".com" at the end of their name. Yet as Blackstone co-founder Stephen Schwarzman has rightly observed, capital is "virtually borderless, flowing around the world in pursuit of opportunity."[40] That capital can move around the world at the proverbial "click of a mouse" is a known quantity today, the notion of "borderless" credit is so well understood that it's almost a cliché, but the crucial truth about it cannot be minimized.

Not only is the truth about global credit frequently forgotten (as an upcoming chapter focused on the Federal Reserve will discuss), but it's perhaps not properly celebrated. Just as "it takes the world" to create things like the Burj, so does it take global credit production to liquefy the abundant commercial activity taking place around the world.

And yes, you read that right. Credit is *created*. As the Mill quote that begins this chapter vivifies, "it is in money that the capital is computed and estimated." No one borrows "money" or seeks "money" as much as they yet again seek the "tangibles" for which money can be exchanged: *resources*. Trucks, tractors, computers, office space, desks, chairs, and most crucial of all, human capital. Yes, credit is created—it's produced. As a corollary to the Adam Smith quote that begins this book, the sole use of money is to move resources to their highest use. Money is the measure flowing around the world, and its rapid movement is a happy signal of resource access flowing to where opportunity is greatest.

In 2001, and as U.S. finance for technology startups was increasingly scarce, PayPal went global in pursuit of capital. Woolway recalled to Soni that in Taipei, "The investors there just loved us . . . even after the downturn . . . They loved the fact that someone from Silicon Valley would come out to Seoul or Taipei."[41] Globalized credit ultimately proved

PayPal's savior. It was in 2001 that PayPal completed a $90 million funding round solely composed of international investors.[42] Please keep in mind that while the technology-laden Nasdaq had soared above 5,000 in March of 2000, by the following March it was below 2,000 and going lower (recall the market action coming out of 9/11). The global funding was the savior and ultimate bridge to PayPal's later IPO, followed by a $1.5 billion acquisition by eBay. What was "impossible" eventually succeeded in rather miraculous fashion. Musk would use the proceeds to fund SpaceX, Tesla, Solar City, and countless other leaps. But those stories have been written.

A snapshot of PayPal's endless funding difficulties that led to accession of foreign capital is provided as a way of reminding readers yet again of the inevitability of money. To be clear, the author is not arguing funding is inevitable— far from it. Galaxies, actually. One of the most insulting notions in the world of finance and economics is the idea of "easy money." There's no such thing—not even close. At the same time, it's useful to point out that if your commercial idea is a good one and you're able to reach investors with it, you're in no way limited by the country of operation when it comes to funding. Since resources are produced globally, so can money be found globally. In the words of Mill, demand and supply of goods and the supply and demand of money "are equivalent expressions."[43] Money in circulation is production determined, at which point the monetary fruits of production flow around the world in pursuit of opportunity.

As the global economy liberalizes, and as more production takes place around the world, investment into U.S. commercial concepts increasingly flows from well outside the U.S. What's true for the U.S., also applies to other countries.

Think Jack Ma, founder of Alibaba, Ant Group, and a variety of other entrepreneurial concepts. Ant has developed some highly innovative digital lending concepts for the Chinese market (or any market for that matter), but as the *Wall Street Journal's* Jing Yang and Julie Steinberg reported in 2021, Ant needed to be domiciled in China to secure licensing so that it could "operate Alipay, its highly popular mobile App." The challenge, according to Yang and Steinberg, was that this arrangement "limited the company's ability to raise funds directly from foreign investors." No problem, it turns out. Again, *money finds the innovative*. Ant raised $10 billion from investors (including U.S. based giants like Silver Lake, T. Rowe Price, and the Carlyle Group) in 2018 via an offshore funding vehicle that made it possible for Ant "to raise funds in dollars."[44]

In response to Ant's globalized capital raise, some might say that anything brought to market by Jack Ma would be an exception given the enormous valuation ($260B) investors have placed on Ma's initial home run, Alibaba. It would on its face read as a fair response, but one not grounded in reality. Indeed, it's not just Ma's genius that's proven a lure for global capital. The simple truth is that investors have long wanted to become involved in financing the technological evolution of a country long on talent but short on investor sophistication, including what business writer Sebastian Mallaby would describe as "two clunky stock exchanges, in Shanghai and Shenzhen." Mallaby indicates that the Silicon Valley funding style of equity investments, preferred stock, and stock options "was novel to the mainland," but seemingly the much bigger obstacle was that the "Chinese government forbade foreign ownership of a broad swath of Chinese businesses, including ones that ran websites." Think, of course, what this meant for pioneering U.S. investment banks (in China) eager to get a piece of companies like Alibaba. U.S. investment was technically *illegal*.

The problem for the Chinese government was that old cliché mentioned earlier in this chapter about money moving to opportunity at a "click of a mouse," or the "borderless" nature of credit that Schwarzman mentioned. Sure enough, and with an eye on breathing "life into China tech, the U.S. venture capitalists (VCs) and their lawyers came up with a series of workarounds." Mallaby reports that "the Chinese Internet companies they backed were incorporated in the Cayman Islands," and "a Cayman outfit could accept investment capital from a non-Chinese VC." To use one of many examples, Mallaby writes that "Goldman Sachs was forbidden to invest in an Internet startup in Hangzhou, but it could buy shares in its Cayman parent."[45]

And it was more than Goldman Sachs showcasing its financial wizardry. Alibaba rival Tencent achieved lift-off in 1998 thanks to a $1.1 million capital infusion from IDG, another U.S. VC. Baidu, yet another China-based Internet giant, secured financing from a fund led by Valley eminence Tim Draper.[46] In the words of Mallaby, "China's technology boom was forged to a remarkable extent by American investors."[47] Put another way, without intrepid flows of capital from the U.S., the Chinese technology boom would likely have exhibited stumbling qualities to this very day.

What's true in China is even truer in Silicon Valley. Mentioned in the previous paragraph was Tim Draper. The initial VC fund he raised with Pitch Johnson had $450,000, only for the two investors to drive across northern California in search of companies with "'electro-' or 'onics'" in the name, after which they would knock on doors in the hopes of meeting a company president.[48] Considering Apple in its early days before going public, British investor Anthony Montagu flew all the way to northern California from London in order to see the company up close. After a few hours at headquarters, Montagu told Apple president Mike Scott that "I brought my overcoat with me, and I have my toothbrush, and I'll just sit in the lobby. I'm not going to leave without acquiring some stock."[49] Amid all the excitement about Internet pioneer Netscape, Mayfield Fund investor Glenn Mueller told Netscape founder Jim Clark that "if you don't let us invest, my partners are going to kill me."[50]

All of which requires a shift to what will close this chapter. There's this notion quite popular in American economic circles that central banks like the Federal Reserve control the fate of U.S. economic activity. Supposedly with their rate fiddling, they can engineer economic growth or its opposite.

Christopher Leonard spells out the simplistic, commonly believed model: "When the Fed raises interest rates, it slows down the economy. When the Fed lowers interest rates, it speeds up the economy."[51] Rare is it that so much confusion can be found in two short sentences. In Leonard's defense, he's not alone—not even close. And the confusion is not endemic to journalists. Within the economics profession, there are several monolithic beliefs. One of them, and it's far from a partisan view, is the unrelentingly foolish conceit of the late Nobel Laureate Milton Friedman that an overly tight Federal Reserve caused the Great Depression. Quoting Ben Bernanke in 2002 while he was giving a speech to an audience that included Friedman, "Regarding the Great Depression. You're right, we did it. We're very sorry. But thanks to you, we won't do it again."[52] Bernanke's quip that elicited great laughter in a room full of economists and media enablers was an admission that the severity of the Depression was the fault of the Fed. No mention of the Smoot-Hawley tariffs that foisted record taxes on 20,000+ foreign goods, of the stupendous increases in federal spending that existed as a huge tax on progress, the increase in the top tax rate to 83 percent, the imposition of injurious taxes of up to 74 percent on retained corporate earnings, of the federal government out-bidding businesses for access to precious labor, or perhaps FDR's decision to devalue the dollar from a fixed rate of $20.67 per ounce of gold to $35; thus signaling to investors eager to put capital to work that any returns would come back in soggier dollars. None of this was mentioned. To economists, the Fed yet again controls the economy's fate, and it allegedly chose decline in the 1930s. Per Leonard, "The Fed's one super-power is its ability to create new dollars and pump them into the banking system,"[53] but apparently the Fed couldn't do enough "pumping" in the 1930s.

It's amazing yet again to witness the grip of the totally nonsensical. That Friedman was so wise, and Bernanke was at least book smart, causes one to wonder. How could they have fallen for such an absurd viewpoint as the Fed playing the insurmountable barrier to credit inflows? Money *always* finds opportunity, without regard for international borders. Attempts by central banks to render credit expensive or cheap, discussed in detail in the next chapter, are toothless relative to existing incentives for the resource-rich to match their capital with the talented. Artificial rates from central banks are intensely meek relative to money flows, as are laws as the experience with Chinese tech reveals in bright colors. What's true in China is true in the U.S.

Consider illegal gambling. Despite its unlawful status, a 2018 report in the *New York Times* estimated that Americans were wagering illegally to the tune of $150 billion annually.[54] As for illegal drugs, many have tried to provide a reasonable estimate of the size of this industry. In May of 2022, the *Wall Street Journal* ran a piece about a "Drug-Smuggling Tunnel Found Linking San Diego to Mexico." Six people were charged with "conspiracy to distribute more than 1,750 pounds of cocaine" transported through a 1,700-foot-long tunnel connecting Tijuana to San Diego.[55] Money necessary to move—yes—market goods to where they're demanded is copious. The "seen" is the arrest; the "unseen" is all the arrests not taking place as finance matches itself with trade that politicians vainly aim to keep illegal. Resources denominated in money always find their way to the returns they seek.

To then believe, as so many economists do, that the Fed could keep global investment from finding its way to what was then the world's most dynamic economy is not serious. An admittedly primitive form of capital (cigarettes) lubricated post-war economic activity in Germany as the previous chapter indicated, yet we're supposed to believe that a central bank projecting its influence through banks that were rapidly losing market share could somehow tighten credit, doesn't rate serious discussion at all. However, this notion of an all-powerful Fed is the consensus today. The good news is that there's nothing to it. The Fed quite simply did not cause the 1930s to happen. More realistically, and as future chapters will demonstrate, reduced "money supply" or lending, was a logical consequence of policies restraining growth, not an allegedly austere Fed.

What was true in the 1930s is even truer today. As of 2014, the banks through which the Fed projects its overstated influence could only claim somewhere in the range of 15 percent of total U.S. lending[56], and even the latter was an overstatement considering what little risk banks are willing to take. The only limit to credit availability is production itself, for the only reason to seek credit is to seek access to actual resources. The Fed can't shrink, nor can it increase the resources that instigate lending, nor can the Fed impede the profit-motivated flow of resources to their highest use. The theory about the Fed causing the Great Depression leaves much to be desired, but as the next chapter will reveal, the notion that the Fed can decree "easy credit," "easy money," or anything of the sort is, put simply, wholly false.

CHAPTER FOUR

THE FEDERAL RESERVE AND THE INSULTING MYTH ABOUT "EASY MONEY"

*"Ask any rich man of common prudence, to which
of the two sorts of people he has lent the greater part
of his stock, to those who, he thinks, will employ it
profitably, or those who will spend it idly, and he
will laugh at you for proposing the question."*
– Adam Smith, *The Wealth of Nations*

"I can't take that offer. I just want the money. I don't want
any points in the movie."

These were the words of actor Donald Sutherland, when offered $20,000 to appear in *Animal House*. In addition to the cash compensation, Sutherland had two percent of the film's box office gross dangled in front of him.[57] Sutherland had low expectations for the film, which explains why he demanded, and received, $35,000 to act in the movie sans any share in earnings from the box office.

Some readers are shaking their heads at Sutherland's lack of foresight, but the future was opaque. Furthermore, Sutherland wasn't the only skeptic. Few of stature wanted anything to do with what wasn't expected to be a memorable movie. Ned Tanen, who was President of Universal Pictures in the mid-1970s, cast his net wide in pursuit of a director willing to take on the project. The problem was that John Schlesinger (*Midnight Cowboy*), Bob Rafelson (*Five Easy Pieces*), Mike Nichols (*The Graduate*), and George Roy Hill (*The Sting*) all passed. And the names listed don't comprise all who were offered the job. Industry speculation to this day is that the offer to direct *Animal House* never even made it past the agents of the directors. Eventually Universal settled on John Landis, but as Landis later observed, "The fact that they hired this kid shows you how unimportant the studio thought this movie was."[58] Chevy Chase thought it so unimportant that he chose to make *Foul Play* instead of playing Eric "Otter" Stratton in the film no one seemed to want anything to do with (Tim Matheson won the part instead).[59] All of this took place before any filming had begun. Inauspicious beginnings to say the least.

The funny thing is that even once the film was shot, there was still skepticism. One of the writers, Harold Ramis, told Landis "You fucked it up!" upon seeing a "rough version" of the movie.[60] As always, the future was so very opaque. It turns out moviegoers and critics saw something in *Animal House* that some of the people very close to it seemingly did not. A movie that cost $3 million to produce went on a run of eight straight weeks as the #1 film in the U.S. on the way to a $140 million gross.[61] For $15,000 in extra salary, Sutherland gave up roughly $2.8 million *in 1978*. Film critic Roger Ebert gave *Animal House* four out of four stars, writing that "The movie is vulgar, raunchy, ribald, and occasionally scatological. It is also the funniest movie comedy since Mel Brooks made *The Producers*."[62]

The critical acclaim *Animal House* garnered along with its notable box office proved valuable to Ramis. He recalled taking a newspaper with a review of the movie to the bank to secure a down payment on a house. "I said to the loan officer, 'Look, I have a piece of this movie. I'm sure I'll be solvent.' That was my collateral. The guy laughed and gave me the loan right there."[63]

The late Ramis's experience with a loan officer is very telling about a greater truth: credit is never easy. At this point readers likely know why credit is hard to obtain—no one borrows money. It will be repeated that when we borrow dollars, we're borrowing real goods and services. Arguably more important is that we're borrowing *time*. Think about the meaning of compound interest, particularly in an economically dynamic country like the United States. "Buy-and-Hold" is a known quantity whereby purchasing the S&P 500 or Nasdaq and forgetting about it has long been the path to steady wealth gains over time. It's a long way of saying credit is never easy or cheap simply because it's *very expensive* to allocate wealth in foolhardy fashion. As the Smith quote that begins this chapter makes plain, the notion of those with wealth blithely loaning it without regard to whom the wealth is being handed over to is just not serious. Money is very serious, which means credit is never cheap.

Despite this truth, there's a persistent narrative of this moment (and in the years and decades before this moment) that says credit is cheap, and that the Federal Reserve is the entity making it so. To offer up one of countless examples from the financial press, in an April 2022 piece for the *Wall Street Journal*, the very excellent columnist Andy Kessler wrote about the years leading up to 2022 as a time when "So many companies were given long runways facilitated by the Federal Reserve's decadelong zero-interest-rate policy, which made capital practically free."[64] The speculation here is that Kessler doesn't believe what he wrote. For one, he made his fortune analyzing technology companies, and eventually investing in them. He's seen up close how fraught is the funding situation for businesses aiming to rewrite the future. Looking back to the previous chapter, and Elon Musk's recollection to *The Founders* author Jimmy Soni that PayPal "was a hard company to keep alive," Kessler more than most would know very well what Musk was up against. Furthermore, it was Kessler who penned a 2017 column for the *Journal* in which he opined that the "dirty little secret of Silicon Valley is that nine out of 10 funded investments fail, often spectacularly so."[65] Not enough about how few technology startups make it? If so, we can turn to Peter Thiel, Musk's partner in PayPal. As he described it in his 2014 book *Zero to One*, "most venture-backed companies don't IPO or get acquired; most fail, usually soon after they start."[66]

The main thing is that Kessler knows the reality of funding in the technology space. Given the failure rate of companies in the most dynamic sector of the world's most dynamic economy, there's no such thing as "easy money" or "easy credit." Which means Kessler has to know that capital has never been anything close to "practically free" for technology businesses simply because to make it so would be for investors to light money on fire with great frequency. They don't operate that way; *money is serious*. Repeat this as many times as needed.

All of which brings us back to Sebastian Mallaby and the "power law" that drives venture investing. To understand this remarkable approach to capital allocation, it's best to think first about the 80/20 principle. In a broad sense, it means a small percentage of causes have outsized effects. For the typical person, it tells us to prioritize the employees, customers, and business lines that will yield the greatest returns. The relatively few move us forward. Think Michael Jordan on the Chicago Bulls. With him, the Bulls won six NBA Championships. Without him, they won zero. Jimmy

Johnson would let Troy Aikman fall asleep in Dallas Cowboy team meetings but cut John Roper for doing the same thing. Look it up . . .

Notable about venture investing is that the 80/20 principle is something more like the 98/2 principle. For just about any venture fund that can claim successful returns, in nearly every instance, grand-slam investments in one or two companies will power returns exponentially greater than what investors would have enjoyed without them. Mallaby cites many examples in his masterful 2022 book *The Power Law*, including the returns achieved in the first venture fund at legendary VC outfit Kleiner Perkins. Mallaby describes it best: "the fourteen investments in the first fund showed a combined profit of $208 million; of that, fully 95 percent came from Tandem and Genentech. Without those two home-run investments, the first fund would have generated a multiple of 4.5x, still comfortably outperforming the return on the S&P 500 over the eleven-year period. With the home runs, the multiple was 42x."[67]

Stop and think about Mallaby's example of the "power law" of venture investing and the popular notion of "easy" or "practically free" capital. There's quite simply no such thing in Silicon Valley. There's no borrowing there by startups at any realistic rate of interest. What would be the point of lending? Who, given a failure rate north of 90 percent, would casually hand over capital for something close to free? Still, the much bigger truth is that no venture capital firm in Silicon Valley (or anywhere for that matter) would ever finance technology companies through debt of any kind simply because the economics of doing so make no sense. Returning to the all-powerful power law yet again, Peter Thiel notes that "The biggest secret in venture capital is that the best investment in a successful fund equals or outperforms the entire rest of the fund."[68] Successful funds aren't made that way via debt finance.

All of which requires more thought in consideration of the Fed. It aims to make lending "easy" or "cheap" through a low federal funds rate, but there's no debt finance to speak of in high-risk locales like Silicon Valley: what investor would lend to startups in return for the income streams of companies that probably won't have any income in the first place? Of course, the bigger reason startups can't attract debt finance is because without equity stakes in companies, the business model for VCs collapses. Refer back to the Thiel quote if you're scratching your head. It's the rare grand slam that papers over all the misses, and much more. There aren't grand slams with debt finance, which means money has never been anywhere close to easy in Silicon Valley. In reality, the cost of capital is staggeringly high.

The highest profile of tens of thousands of examples would be Apple. When Steve Jobs initially began his search for funding in the 1970s, he offered a New York City computer store owner 10 percent of the company for $10,000.[69] Another investor who had initially hit it big with Intel stock options, Mike Markkula, purchased 26 percent of Apple from Jobs for $91,000. When Apple eventually floated its shares in December of 1980, it was the largest IPO since Ford Motor Company's in 1956. The valuation was $1.8 billion. Readers can do the math as a way of understanding how expensive it was for Jobs to acquire Markkula's capital.[70]

As of this writing, Cisco's market valuation is $197 billion. Don Valentine, seen by some as the grandfather of Silicon Valley venture capital, purchased 33 percent of Cisco for $2.5 million.[71] To be clear for readers who are shaking their heads, odds were extraordinarily high that Valentine and his investors were going to lose everything. Remember the words of Andy Kessler earlier in this chapter: "nine out of 10 funded investments fail, often spectacularly so." The high ratio of losers to winners speaks not just to why capital is so expensive in technology, but it's similarly true that the rare grand slams also explain expensive capital. That they're "grand slams" is the signal of just how few investors think these companies have a chance in startup phase. If their prospects were seen as good, capital would be much cheaper to access.

To all this, some will respond that the companies mentioned are older; that with the potential for technology investments more of a known quantity today, the cost of capital is less. Except that it's hard to make that case. Google did a capital raise in 1999 at a time when capital flows into Silicon Valley were surging, but VC legend John Doerr still paid $12 million for 12.5 percent of the would-be search giant,[72] Goldman Sachs paid $5 million for half of Alibaba in 1999 (oh, the regret the Firm must have for selling *way* too early),[73] Peter Thiel famously purchased 10 percent of Facebook for $500,000 in 2004,[74] and in 2010 Benchmark Capital and Bill Gurley purchased 20 percent of Uber for $12 million.[75] Today Uber is worth nearly $50 billion. Facebook is worth $440 billion, and that's after a big market correction. To repeat, the business model of venture capital tautologically demands that capital be extraordinarily expensive. This would be true even if there were a market for debt finance at rates of interest close to 100 percent. Even then, and in consideration of how many startups go under, the vast majority of debt deals in a hypothetical scenario would prove worthless rather quickly. As for the "grand slams," returns on debt versus equity are exceedingly small by comparison, which means the losers in VC funds would always drown out the very few winners.

Of course, as readers know, the Fed strives vainly to keep the cost of borrowing cheap. In other words, what the Fed does has absolutely nothing to do with the cost of credit in Silicon Valley. Still, it has meaning—just not what people think.

To understand the meaning of the Fed's actions, it's fair to say that it has no credit to give out, expand, or to make "easy." Credit is produced in the real economy; no one borrows money. Still, what are readers to think of the Fed's fiddling with overnight lending rates among banks at or close to zero percent? Does this perhaps make credit "easy" for corporations not in Silicon Valley? The answer yet again is no. Markets always speak their piece. No doubt politicians can decree that market goods be cheap (think vain attempts at "rent control" in Manhattan), but ultimately prices will find their level; that or the supply of what's decreed cheap will shrink.

Applied to the Fed and its allegedly low rates, the result is merely a re-affirmation of abundant credit for corporations already swimming in credit options. To see the emptiness of the Fed's attempts at economic relevance, it's useful to return to Christopher Leonard's *The Lords of Easy Money* and a quote for the ages from the always self-unaware former Chairman of the Federal Reserve, Ben Bernanke.

It was 2013 and the Fed was in pursuit of the impossibility that is "easy money" via quantitative easing. During a FOMC gathering, Leonard reports that Dallas Fed president Richard Fisher "gave a long, impassioned speech against Bernanke's push deeper and deeper into interventions." Fisher then got specific. He referenced a recent call with the CFO of Texas Instruments (TI), in which the executive explained what it would do with the $1.5 billion it borrowed at interest rates ranging from 0.45 percent to 1.6 percent. What Fisher stressed the most was that as opposed to putting the borrowed funds to work, TI was buying shares of its own stock; shares that paid a 2.5 percent dividend.[76] About the financial maneuver, it reads to the author as funny simply because it sounds like TI was buying its own stock so that it could pay itself dividends from its own treasury. Except that a focus on what TI did with the money is a distraction.

This example is brought up for reasons unrelated to whether those borrowing "cheaply" were building factories, hiring engineers, or merely buying back stock. Again, actions taken with allegedly "costless" credit miss the point. What's useful about the TI example is that the company has a market capitalization of $172 billion. The latter is worth more than a few seconds of thought. In thinking about the company's valuation, there's really no mystery about its ability to borrow in large amounts at low rates. *Of course it can.* While there are no sure things in life, let's agree that TI could qualify as a low-risk borrower—particularly in the context of a $1.5 billion loan relative to its valuation.

Then, let's think about the cost of borrowing for TI in relation to the financing of startups by venture investors. Mallaby writes that this intrepid form of finance was "originally dubbed adventure capital." From there, Mallaby wrote the idea behind "adventure capital" was "to back technologists who were too dicey and speculative to get a conventional bank loan but who promised the chance of a resounding payoff to investors with a taste for audacious invention."[77] Well, there you have it. The capital made available to the outsiders aggressively pursuing an entirely different commercial future would have to be extraordinarily expensive to rate capital commitments in the first place. There's quite simply no debt finance out there for the dreamers ever in pursuit of the outlandish, impossible, or both. Again, the Fed is a non-factor in the parts of the economy where dynamism and vision are most rewarded.

Fair enough, but what about the established parts of the economy? What about the parts of the economy readily financed by the banks through which the Fed projects its influence? Hopefully TI answers the question. The paradoxical truth vivified by TI is that borrowing rates at banks are low precisely because credit at those banks is extraordinarily *tight*, albeit in a different way. Banks will lend at low rates simply because they're making loans to individuals and corporations so well collateralized that they don't really need the money. Or if they do need the money, the options for cheap credit are endless. Does anyone seriously think that absent the Fed's rate interventions made to make credit cheap that TI would suddenly be paying a much higher market rate? The question answers itself.

The banks that the Fed projects its overstated influence through are lending to individuals and companies at rates that are "practically free" (Kessler) simply because they're not taking any kind of risk with the funds deposited with them. Put another way, there's a saying that banks make loans to entities that don't need the loans. Precisely. With venture capital investing, it can't be said enough that the capital must be equity finance, expensive, and wholly without regard to the Fed's rate fiddling. Expensive capital is what makes audacious bets on tomorrow's potential innovators possible. Conversely, bank lending at low rates of interest by its very descriptor must steer well clear of the dreamers. The banking model would similarly collapse if debt finance were directed to the companies of tomorrow. There's no "easy money" from banks simply because banks, as their low borrowing charges indicate, cannot lend to those actually in need of capital.

What does all this mean for the Fed? In addition to clarifying the lie that is "easy money" or "easy credit" or "costless" credit, ideally it shows how toothless the Fed is to influence much of anything. It's a legend in its own mind, which is why Bernanke's reply to Fisher's impassioned talk against QE is so entertaining and sad at the same time. In reply, Bernanke remarkably told Fisher (it's difficult to type this without laughing) that "I know we put a lot of value on anecdotal reports around this table, and often to great credit. But I do want to urge you to not overweight the macroeconomic opinions of private-sector people who are not trained in economics."[78] You can't make this up!

To the readers of this chapter still wedded to convention and the view that the Fed is powerful enough to dissuade you from the chapter's conclusions, please re-read Bernanke's quote. If you don't believe my reasoning, think deeply about what Bernanke claimed and how it embodies thought inside the Federal Reserve. Having done that, ask yourself: would the U.S. economy be anything like its incredibly vibrant self if the "geniuses" like Bernanke were actually powerful? The Fed is not the story, and it never was. This certain truth will become more apparent as we move to the next chapters and address the almost-religious belief that central banks can increase so-called "money supply" just by "pumping" money into the "system," or decrease it just the same.

CHAPTER FIVE

THERE'S NO SUCH THING AS "MONEY SUPPLY", THERE'S ONLY PRODUCTION

"No individual and no nation need fear at any
time to have less money than it needs."
– Ludwig von Mises, *The Theory of Money and Credit*

In the 1850s, foreign banks began to dock at China's commercial ports. Their purpose was to finance the increasingly bustling economic activity within the country. Though Chinese officialdom didn't initially resist the arrival of foreign finance, monetary historian Eswar Prasad reports in his 2017 book *Gaining Currency* that they eventually questioned the development based on the view that foreign money "was becoming the basis of commerce."[79] There wasn't much leadership could do, however. Global financial flows invariably overpower efforts to limit them; money naturally finds the productive because it has no other purpose than moving resources to higher uses. As we'd see again in the twenty-first century, capital owners discovered that projects of enterprising minds on the mainland constituted a highly productive use.

Ironically enough, one of the most crucial sources of Chinese finance had origins in Middle East centuries before. As Jonathan Kaufman wrote in his 2020 book *The Last Kings of Shanghai*, the two most important names in the funding of Chinese growth were Jewish families with origins in Baghdad, who didn't speak Chinese: The Sassoons and the Kadoories.

While Jews had "always lived at the margins of society in Europe," they had "flourished in Baghdad" according to Kaufman. The regions differed at a macro level too; while Europe was "mired in the darkness of the Middle Ages, Baghdad was one of the most cosmopolitan cities in the world."[80] It's a reminder of the simple truth that prosperity is driven by people. Where the creative are free to flourish, prosperity follows simply because freedom is the lure for the ultimate capital: human. Keep this in mind with reference to Baghdad today. Could a wise central bank "pumping money" into the economy make it prosperous?

Returning to the Sassoons, the family could claim prominence in Baghdad going back over 800 years. In 1829, 37-year-old David Sassoon exited Baghdad after the city's Turkish officials threatened to hang him over a tax bill. He made his way to India, where he "helped found the Bank of Bombay" and began the family's fruitful move into China. It truly took flight when Sassoon's second son, Elias, embarked on a 70-day voyage up the Chinese coast. He had capital in hand, helping the Bank of Bombay grow market share by "financing shipments of opium and textiles" and separately "offering loans to smaller merchants."[81] It was apparent all the way from Bombay that there was opportunity in China for the Sassoons, which led to an expansion.

David Sassoon eventually decided that loan approval from bankers in Bombay and London was not moving quickly enough. The Sassoons couldn't just be visitors in China; they needed permanency there to grow the franchise. David sent Arthur Sassoon to Hong Kong, and he eventually joined with other financiers in creating Hongkong and Shanghai Bank.[82] Now "globally systemically important" according to bank regulators, the bank still operates today under its modern moniker, HSBC. The expansion, and commitment to permanency, would ultimately prove wise.

The Kadoories could similarly claim Baghdad origins. Elly Kadoorie lacked the pedigree of the various Sassoons, but made up for it with towering ambition. Elly left Baghdad when he was fifteen and found his way to Bombay where his apprenticeship with the Sassoons began. He rose quickly and soon enough worked in Hong Kong. A dispute over a barrel of disinfectant that Elly provided on credit amid a plague got him on the wrong side of the Sassoons such that he resigned, but Kaufman is clear that Elly had already "decided it was time to strike out on his own."[83] Elly requires discussion not only due to his remarkable success, but also for the subsequent achievements of his son, Lawrence Kadoorie, in Shanghai. In Lawrence's words, "There never was and there never will be another city like Shanghai between the two wars." The Sassoons and Kadoories prospered in concert with Shanghai's leap into the A-list category of global cities. The wildly sophisticated Victor Sassoon had massive holdings in Shanghai and beyond, and created the extremely luxurious Cathay Hotel,[84] which still stands today as the Peace Hotel. Elly and son Lawrence lived at Marble Hall, a structure "twice the size of any existing home in Shanghai" and maintained by forty-two servants.[85]

What explains this prosperity? No doubt China had a long history of commerce well before the nineteenth and twentieth centuries that was increasingly matched with capital. But it's worth stressing that Shanghai was a very *open* city; one that didn't require a visa to enter. Think about what this meant between the wars, and in particular once Adolf Hitler rose to power. Shanghai became a destination for Jewish people escaping persecution. The sign that awaited some of them read as follows: WELCOME TO SHANGHAI. YOU ARE NO LONGER JEWS BUT CITIZENS OF THE WORLD. ALL SHANGHAI WELCOMES YOU.

Notable about the above is that the man financing the migration of many Jewish refugees was none other than Victor Sassoon.[86] By 1939, Kaufman reports that 1,000 refugees were arriving in the city each month[87] and often bringing with them impressive business know-how. Think about this in terms of Victor Sassoon and Lawrence Kadoorie. The growth in Shanghai that was making them staggeringly rich was born of talented people. People are always and everywhere the economy, and where there's human capital it's a given that financial capital will be abundant.

However, the talent influx brought up an odd paradox. It could be argued that the abundant wealth creation that followed gave life to the collectivist leanings that eventually destroyed what was so grand. Visible wealth gives those who desire something for nothing the props with which to galvanize the gullible about wealth redistribution. Mao himself organized the communist party not far from the splendor of China's grandest mansions.[88] Too, Shanghai's openness to those escaping persecution both set the stage for its renaissance and prefigured the Second World War that would destroy all that the Sassoons and Kadoories had created. Hitler's expansionary plans became apparent in the late 1930s and Victor Sassoon concluded that the Japanese had plans for Asia similar to Germany's in Europe. He kept his foresight from his employees, however, as he did not "want them to know how depressed [he was]."[89] The problem was that Sassoon didn't liquidate based on his pessimism about China's future. He held on, only for the communists to eventually relieve him of over $500 million worth of property.[90] While Sassoon hung on until he was substantially dispossessed, Kaufman writes that "Throughout the 1930s, the Kadoories had become wary of Shanghai and poured more and more of their money 700 miles south into Hong Kong."[91] This set the less prominent of the two families up for much greater preeminence in later generations.

Mao Zedong gradually gained control in the aftermath of the war. There will be no attempt to provide a history of the tragic rise of Mao and the communists in China, as countless other books offer detailed accounts. A theory will be presented in its place. The more obvious drivers of the communist embrace are the ones previously mentioned regarding wealth as a visible target for redistribution, and the leadership vacuums left by the Second World War. However, a factor often overlooked involves the currency—China's was destroyed.

Put another way, socialism or communism reached China well before Mao took over. For what is devaluation but a horrid taking of wealth, and realistically a redistribution of it? What does devaluation instigate among those holding money? It encourages consumption over savings that are directed to entrepreneurs and businesses looking to create a better future. It's all a statement of the obvious—but the obvious requires routine emphasis given the belief among economists that devaluation is stimulative. Wealth redistribution (think socialism) is logically devastating. Considering China's tragic devaluation, let's examine the numbers.

In 1944, twenty Chinese dollars were exchangeable for $1. Two years later, $1 could be purchased with 2,000 Chinese dollars. In 1947, 12,000 Chinese dollars bought a dollar. Not long after that, Kaufman writes that "the black-market rate was a million to one."[92] The story of China's devaluation requires a quick digression. There's a view that won't die which says government debt brings on currency devaluation. In shortened fashion, "deficits cause inflation." The view is hard to take seriously, as it implies that investors would readily line up to buy debt that will be paid back in money that buys progressively less. Markets aren't that stupid despite what dominant ideologies would have you believe.

At the same time, it's fair to point out that governments sometimes move in a collectivist direction, only to rob the people of their wealth through devaluation. It happened in China in a gruesome way. As John Maynard Keynes once asserted, currency devaluation "discredits enterprise" as so many see their savings destroyed. People save for a better tomorrow in that they shift the monetary fruits of their work to others now in return for more money in the future. They save for what their savings can be exchanged for in the future. When devaluation strikes, their efforts suddenly prove foolish, and they're wiped out. On the horror of devaluation, Keynes most famously wrote that "There is no subtler, surer means of overturning the existing basis of society than to debauch the currency. The process engages all the hidden forces of economic law on the side of destruction, and it does it in a manner which not one man in a million is able to diagnose."

One could argue that the Keynes quotes are excessive here. But in response, who isn't bothered by theft? Is it any surprise that amid the theft of devaluation a sick person like Mao might attract a following that he wouldn't otherwise? No doubt wealth creation gives voice to the demagogues looking to redistribute it, but arguably the biggest instigator of collectivism is the *taking* of the common man's wealth.

It's all a long way of asserting that China's mid-twentieth century descent into communism was arguably driven by monetary error, at which point there's a money story that follows. Indeed, while Shanghai was the Paris of the Orient in between the wars, the post-war rise of Mao repelled the commercial talent who made the country great. Kaufman notes that as China committed suicide, 100,000 of Shanghai's best and brightest took their talents to Hong Kong.[93] Capital followed, as one would expect, since it has no purpose where talent isn't located or where it's not allowed to flourish. Looked at in historical terms, it's popular to say that Hong Kong's economic freedom was transformational. There's no argument with that. It was the freedom that proved the lure for so many of Shanghai's vital few. At the same time, it must be stressed that *Shanghai's vital few* moved to Hong Kong. Read the previous sentence a few more times. People are the source of economic progress, and the people who made Shanghai incomparable between the wars had taken their genius to Hong Kong. Is it any wonder that capital followed them? The people were the wealth, and they left.

Some are wondering why all the proverbial throat clearing about the Sassoons and Kadoories in a chapter about the so-called "money supply." Their stories elucidate a foundational point: money exists in the locus of the productive. The story of these two remarkable families who brilliantly financed Chinese growth (despite, as previously mentioned, not even knowing Chinese[94]) reveals this truth. And in thinking about the arrival of the Sassoons in China, it's useful to contemplate their pursuit of fortune with the popular notion about central banks very much in mind. It is so often assumed that the Fed can "stimulate" the economy with interest rate cuts as though the Fed is the source of capital without which growth cannot occur. More realistically, capital is *produced,* and it migrates to where it will be treated well. In other words, the story of the Sassoons and the Kadoories is an explanation of how economic growth actually works.

While business journalists promote the impressively obtuse viewpoint that economic growth occurs via the permission of central bankers, the migrations of the Sassoons and Kadoories remind us yet again that central banks are irrelevant. The surest indicator of economic growth is the arrival of the most commercially talented people. And we know where they're going simply because investors eager to expand their wealth follow them. China beckoned for the Sassoons and eventually the Kadoories because there was business genius to be financed in the country. It wasn't low interest rates that instigated Shanghai's renaissance; it was intrepid finance from outside China that was directed toward the able inside. And when Mao chose to suffocate commercial genius, what made Shanghai remarkable transported itself 700 miles down the coast to Hong Kong.

Yet economists and their enablers in the media focus on central banks and their targeting of overnight lending rates. Pick up any newspaper any day, and the narrative that growth is essentially bestowed on us by benevolent central bankers prevails. As this book is being written in June of 2022, the Federal Reserve is in the midst of "rate hikes" that have journalists and economists on pins and needles. They wear their ignorance garishly. We read on the day this chapter is being written a report from *New York Times* Fed reporter Jeanna Smialek about a cooling labor market in the future. This is "a near certainty as the Federal Reserve Board raises interest rates."[95] Can Smialek really believe that economic vitality is a gift of the Fed? To this question some will doubtless reply along the lines of "this is what they teach in schools today." The response is wanting, as common sense can't be taught. What's lacking among economists and those reporting on them is common sense.

Who could actually believe that central banks decide from the proverbial "commanding heights" how much or how little growth there will be? Such a view implies that the twentieth century, when central planning gave us economic disasters in countries like China, Cuba, and the Soviet Union, never happened. It's not that there weren't wildly smart people in power in the three countries mentioned, but the genius of one, or several, or thousands in power can never match up to the total knowledge of freely acting individuals. Markets work because they incorporate the knowledge and decisions of everyone over the few. Despite this, readers of most economics reporting must read a very slight variation of what journalists naïvely repeat about the Federal Reserve.

What these reporters and economists miss is the beautiful truth that the only closed economy is the global economy. In this global economy, resources are produced. Rising credit is the consequence of this production. The production is directed to its perceived highest uses, or highest uses in terms of the desired risk and growth parameters of investors. Readers know from the previous chapter that in twenty-first century China, the country's technological growth has been closely associated with American finance. In the nineteenth and twentieth centuries, some of the biggest names in Chinese finance had origins in Baghdad. It wasn't the People's Bank of China funding Shanghai's ascendance, but instead courageous financiers who didn't speak Chinese. Finance, in the truest sense of the word, is global.

All of which brings us to the present in the United States, and back to Sebastian Mallaby's brilliant history of venture capital, *The Power Law*. Mallaby writes that as of 2020, "more than 480 'unicorns' boast valuations of more than $1 billion."[96] Of these "unicorns," it's no stretch to say that most are based in California. According to Mallaby, from 2004 to 2019 "California's share of U.S. venture fundraising jumped from 44 percent to 62 percent."[97] Is this the Fed's doing? Is it "easy money?" The Fed-focused claim that the Fed's rate machinations affect valuations via the cost of capital, but valuation in a sector of the economy defined by overwhelming failure, misses the point. As VC legend Tom Perkins has explained, "you succeed in venture capital by backing the right deals, not by haggling over valuations."[98]

It's a long way of saying that an immense amount of investment capital has found its way to California not because the Fed prefers Palo Alto to Clarksburg, West Virginia, but because talent abounds in Palo Alto. Much as the Sassoons and Kadoories focused their financing on Shanghai over Kashgar (the Chinese city that borders Afghanistan), investors today direct a lot of capital to northern California because that's where a lot of technological genius is clustered. The Fed is a non-story.

On the other hand, global capital is a growing story in northern California. Repeat as many times as needed that credit is borderless, that money goes where it's treated well and other truisms. As countries around the world move further away from the central planning that defined the twentieth century, the amount of capital searching for good treatment grows. Please think about this in terms of the Fed. Even if it were true that the Fed's vain attempts at market intervention shrunk the "money supply" inside U.S. banks, it's not as though the U.S. is some autarkic island in terms of investment. Global investors are endlessly in search of ways to put their money to work stateside. What the Fed could allegedly take would be made up for globally.

Consider Masayoshi Son, who initially made his fortune with a software distribution company by the name of SoftBank. Mallaby writes that Son had "acquired a reputation for raising and committing funds extraordinarily quickly." While in pursuit of Yahoo! in 1995, Son immediately said yes to co-founders David Filo and Jerry Yang's valuation of the company at $40 million, only to invest more than half of the $5 million Yahoo! raised. In the next funding round, Son shocked the founders with his quick offer of $100 million in funding in return for 30 percent. "Jerry, everyone needs $100 million," is what Son reportedly said. Son was also quick at raising funds, including talking "$45 billion out of Saudi Arabia's crown prince in the space of forty-five minutes."[99] Son has made and lost a lot of money with his high-profile capital commitments from Yahoo! to Alibaba to WeWork. The point here is that any locale populated with a lot of entrepreneurial talent will have capital from all over the world trying to find its way in.

In 2009 Gideon Yu, CFO of Facebook, got a call from Moscow. It was Russian Internet entrepreneur Yuri Milner. Milner had a romantic view of all things United States and very much wanted to invest in Facebook. That he did is a reminder of yet again of how capital finds interesting commercial ideas from all points global, as opposed to it being released by central bankers. Notable here is that the Facebook of 2009 was in the position to be very choosy about its investors. Investment bankers were *competing* to finance the super-unicorn and investors likewise competed for top spots.

Milner courted Facebook and Mark Zuckerberg for the right to buy private shares in the company, including waiving any demands for a board seat or the right to vote his shares. Milner's DST ultimately purchased a nearly two percent piece of the company for $200 million.[100]

On their own, these anecdotes are just little tidbits picked up from lots of reading. But they speak to something bigger about finance—money finds the brilliant. If you have a good business idea, money is a given. No amount of alleged Fed "tightening" can alter this truth. At the same time, the money that can be abundant in pursuit of talent can also be fickle. Business journalists would have us believe that the Fed chooses not just *when* to expand economic activity through rate cuts, but also when to slow economic activity via rate hikes. Such a view isn't serious. The happy, pro-growth reality is that market-disciplined investors pull away the proverbial "punch bowl," not central bankers.

Consider a front-page story in the *Wall Street Journal* from May of 2022. It reported that "Highflying startups have been grounded, swiftly, by the new climate: layoffs, skeptical investors, an exodus of funds and the prospects of a valuation haircut."[101] Such is life in relentlessly capitalistic northern California. Given the failure rate among technology firms, they're quickly put on a tight leash by their investors as their short and long-term prospects begin to dim.

Thinking about all this in a broader economic sense, if Silicon Valley businesses are in trouble the pain will extend well beyond them. It will be felt around the U.S., and realistically around the world. Technology businesses on their own powerfully enhance business productivity, not to mention how much economic activity around the U.S. (and world) is fueled by what happens in northern California.

One imagines that the response of a typical business reporter or economist to VC tightening would involve the Fed and how many interest-rate cut "bullets" it may have to "kickstart" a lagging economy. Should the Fed reduce interest rates or increase so-called "money supply" to boost the spirits of "skeptical investors" while reversing "the exodus of funds" reported by the *Journal*? Try not to laugh. For one, global market forces would powerfully overwhelm any central bank efforts to reverse the outflow of funds—it wouldn't be a contest. What meager amounts of credit or "money supply" that the Fed could supply Valley banks would be dwarfed by investors feverishly shrinking their exposure.

But wait, some will say. The Fed can go to zero! It can make credit costless, don't you know? Except that the Fed can do no such thing. A producer of no credit itself, the Fed can't decree costless what it doesn't produce. The surest sign that the Fed's zero rate fantasies have no real-world relevance is the business and startup culture in Silicon Valley. Think back to Chapter Four. If the Fed can decree credit free, as many routinely claim, why do Valley startups routinely hand over large equity positions to venture capitalists in return for cash? Rather than give up equity, wouldn't they just take on debt for free? They would certainly like to, but as should be obvious there's not much of a debt market for businesses with a failure rate over 90 percent. That there's no debt finance in Silicon Valley is the surest signal to those interested in reason that the Fed's power to influence much of anything is the stuff of clueless academic economists and journalists, not something to seriously contemplate. No doubt, economists buy into the Fed's importance. Why wouldn't they? The Fed is their patron. No doubt, journalists buy into the Fed as all powerful planner of economic outcomes. Why wouldn't they? This is what economists tell them.

The good news is that reason ultimately intrudes on the fabulist thinking of the overeducated. Actual market forces *always* have their say. Prosperity can't be legislated, or forced, because it's a consequence of freely flowing capital. And unless capital can exit dicey situations (think again of the failure rate in Silicon Valley), it can't enter them either. No amount of Fed fiddling will deter an investment exodus from the Valley, nor can the same central bank restrain an inevitable return of funds in search of the next "unicorns." Global credit flows to where the best and brightest are, but it also departs. The Fed cannot reverse these market truths and thank goodness it can't. Silicon Valley is prosperous not because all its businesses succeed; rather it's prosperous precisely because most don't. Bad ideas fail quickly, thus releasing crucial human and physical capital plus finance to invest in perceived better options. Stasis is the enemy of progress, and Silicon Valley is the antithesis of stasis.

In thinking about all this, it's useful to look back to this chapter's beginning. There it was noted how Baghdad was once one of the world's foremost cities. Was it because there were good central bankers showering "easy money" on the city? Readers know the answer. Baghdad thrived because it was populated by the talented. Fast forward to the present. Could wise central bankers lift Baghdad's economy today by "pumping" so-called "money supply" into the city's banks? Lots of luck there. For a many reasons, Baghdad no longer resembles its former self. Assuming the pumping of billions into Baghdad, the money would depart as quickly as it arrived. Contrary to what you read, and what we're told, money can't be increased in a chosen locale as much as money in circulation soars in one populated by the industrious.

Money is a consequence of brilliance. Money finds the brilliant as opposed to central bank fiddling making money abundant. Central bankers couldn't make Baghdad prosperous and bursting with money any more than the St. Louis Fed could pump "money supply" into East St. Louis to lift it up. Only skilled people can boost "money supply," and the Fed has no ability to multiply people or tell them where to go. Money flows signal the flow of crucial resources and that's not something the Fed can enhance or restrain.

CHAPTER SIX

INFLATION IS NOT "TOO MUCH MONEY CHASING TOO FEW GOODS"

*"As the whole of the goods in the market compose the
demand for money, so the whole of the money constitutes
the demand of goods. The money and goods are seeking
each other for the purpose of being exchanged. They are
reciprocally supply and demand to one another."*
– John Stuart Mill, *Principles of Political Economy*

In the early 1920s, the value of the German mark was
in freefall. It's likely you're already aware of the storied

German hyperinflation. The post-WWI devaluation of the mark is arguably the most famous devaluation of all. Naturally it was overseen by government.

Still, not all manifest explanations are wasteful. Though obvious once spelled out, the circumstances of the German hyperinflation provide an opportunity to dispense with one of the more ridiculous myths about money: central banks as the "money printing" instigators of inflation. Without defending central banks for even a second, such a view about them isn't serious. It's shortsighted and incomplete for a variety of reasons, but the main reason has to do with the fact that devaluation is as old as money itself—certainly as old as government-issued money. As monetary historian Nathan Lewis has put it, "Governments have always debased, devalued, and floated their currencies."[102]

A trip back to the seventh century B.C. provides helpful context. The Turkish Lydia spawned in this era are believed to be the original coins. Notable about the coins is that the gold and silver content in them didn't measure up to their decreed value. Centuries later, Roman emperor Nero desired certain extravagances that the money in his coffers couldn't obtain, only for him to quietly add copper to coins billed as silver.[103] Despite such shenanigans, markets always shine a bright light on efforts to trick them. Nero fooled no one, nor did Turkish monetary authorities, nor have governments fooled anyone since.

That they haven't is kind of a statement of the obvious, but as stated throughout this book, what's obvious requires regular stating: money is just the measure enabling the real exchange of products for products. Money's purpose as a measure is what keeps market actors attuned to changes in its value or hidden attempts toward that end. Producers prefer not to be ripped off. Governments, on the other hand, want something for nothing, and sometimes seek it through devaluation, transferring their largesse and debts to the citizenry.

Governments devalue. Period. To focus on central banks isn't just shortsighted given the history of governments with money; it's also misplaced because the pretense assumes central banks are a powerful and mysterious *other* intent on destroying money, "the little guy" and everything else. No doubt, central bankers relish the views of their critics—the disdain hands them unearned swagger and charisma. The "maestros" have the whole world in their hands, right? Not so fast. In reality, central banks are entities full of hapless economists endlessly stalked by fallacy. Note too that central banks are outsourced arms of government—they're not *other* at all. They're entities formed by elected officials to implement policies politicians either don't know how to enact or don't want to be seen enforcing. In the United States, the Fed is an outsourced function of Congress. Central banks are government and to tie currency devaluation to them is to miss the point and misunderstand history.

As for the model case of Germany, the best guess as to why its devaluation is so well known to even casual followers of history seems connected to a famous image. To feed his family, a middle-aged man comes to market with a wheelbarrow full of marks and little in the way of hope. By December of 1923, the mark had fallen so precipitously that $1 could be exchanged on the open market for 4,200,000,000,000 marks. So much had the currency been destroyed that transactions required literal wheelbarrows full of the currency, or so the story goes. Images are far more powerful than words.

Of course, the image belied the actual truth of what had become of the mark. In a commercial sense, it had already disappeared. Keynes knew this or alluded to this in *A Tract on Monetary Reform*. When money is losing value, individuals "employ foreign money in many transactions where it would have been more natural and convenient to use their own."[104] In his classic, tragic 1975 book about the German monetary disaster, *When Money Dies*, Adam Fergusson wrote of the "scarcity of money"[105] denominated in marks that really shouldn't surprise anyone willing to approach money in a sober manner. To achieve clarity, readers would have to free themselves of all the thoughtless talk about the Fed and other central banks "gunning the money supply" or the Fed using its "one superpower" to "create new dollars and pump them into the banking system" as Christopher Leonard described.[106] Goodness, even if the Fed could exercise this "one superpower," doing so would have no meaning. Money has no purpose absent production. Its "supply" can't be "pumped" or "forced" or anything else commonly relayed.

Thinking about this in terms of Germany, that the number of marks in circulation shrunk is a tautology. Of course they did. They did because underlying all purchases is products for products. Never forget that no one buys with money—they purchase with their production. The money we accept in return for our work, and that we subsequently take out of our pockets to fulfill our consumption desires, is accepted in return for real goods and services simply because that same money will be accepted by other producers in return for their goods and services. The mark disappeared because it no longer was useful as a measure capable of facilitating actual exchange. The wheelbarrow imagery creates the false notion of marks in stupendous amounts being brought to market for goods and services, but the more realistic imagery can be found on the cover of the 2010 re-issue of Fergusson's book: the mark had become nothing more than *litter*. Marks could be found on the streets, and were swept up by street sweepers, but could not be found in cash registers. Well, *of course*. Marks were no longer money. Money commands goods and services. It never lies on the street untaken for long, whereas the mark wasn't worth picking up.

The story of the mark's collapse explains quite a lot. As a brief background, Germany's Bank Law of 1875 required that gold back one-third of all marks issued. There's this myth among critics of gold-defined money that the latter requires gold discoveries to allow currency in circulation to increase. They don't understand what it is they're criticizing, nor do they understand why gold has long been used to define money in the first place.

The worth of gold is not defined by its limited supply or the difficulty of mining it. Gold's worth as money is rooted in the eighteenth and nineteenth century political economist David Ricardo's observation that "there is probably no commodity subject to fewer variations."[107] Readers are sensing a theme. Think back to John Stuart Mill: gold and silver are the commodities "least influenced by any of the causes which produce fluctuations of value." Money is ideal when it's *quiet*, that is, when its value doesn't move. Gold attained global monetary status precisely because of its stability. The existing, above ground stock of gold is exponentially greater than new discoveries, or sales of the metal. Think of it this way: what if you owned a million shares of ExxonMobil only to sell them. Would your sale move the price? Not likely. There are *4.27 billion* shares outstanding of XOM. Your massive holding is quite small relative to the total. Gold's constancy as a measure results from the total stock versus flow scenario that resembles the ExxonMobil example.

Gold doesn't limit the alleged supply of money as much as gold *anchors* the value of money. Gold imbues the measure with stability as opposed to it limiting what's in circulation. To use a broad U.S. example, from 1775 to 1900 the U.S. dollar was defined in terms of gold at a fixed rate of $20.67 an ounce. During that time, dollars in circulation rose roughly 163 times. Obviously, dollars in circulation rose substantially more than gold was discovered, all of which speaks to the foolishness of the criticisms suggesting commodity standards limit money in circulation. No serious economic or monetary thinker would strive to limit the "supply" of a monetary measure—there's no need. What controls "supply" or quantity of money in circulation is people and production. Where production takes place, there will always be money; where production lacks, money will be scarce. So-called "money supply" is a natural market phenomenon as opposed to a central bank phenomenon whereby allegedly wise minds inside grandiose buildings match supply and demand for "money." Gold once again is a way to provide the consequence of production with stability as a measure to enable as much exchange as possible.

Applied to Germany's Bank Law of 1875 that required one-third of marks in circulation to be backed by gold, it's worth pointing out that a gold-defined currency realistically requires no gold backing. If market actors trust the definition such as the dollar pegged to gold at $20.67 an ounce, they would have no reason to exchange money for gold. Why would they? Gold just *is*, while money can be saved at a rate of interest, can be invested and is easier to use as a medium of exchange. Considering that from 1775 to 1900 U.S. dollars in circulation soared 163 times, it's not as though the U.S. had a major gold stock to back the dollar. The dollar's broad circulation was a consequence of its definition in terms of gold. The gold stock that the U.S. federal government owns now results at least in part from the Franklin Delano Roosevelt administration confiscating private holdings of gold in 1933.[108]

While Germany had a gold definition for the mark that was backed by a gold rule, the rule was suspended in 1914.[109] Thus began a slow devaluation of the mark that eventually turned into a rout. Fergusson's remarkably sad book reported that prior to the mark's collapse, a bank clerk could "aspire to a maximum yearly salary of 12,000 marks, but by 1922 the weekly minimum cost to feed a family of four was 2,300 to 2,800 marks."[110] By August of 1923, "most firms gave raises to their employees ranging from 5 million to 15 million marks a week."[111]

Again, the mark was cascading toward nothingness, which made the currency stop circulating as it had previously. To exchange tangible goods and services for a measure in freefall was to get much less in return. Though marks were increasingly unacceptable, dollar holders were treated in a princely fashion. Fergusson recounts the experience of German citizen Hans-George von der Osten. In possession of an American dollar inside Germany in early 1923, he "got hold of six friends and went to Berlin one evening determined to blow the lot; but early the next morning, long after dinner, and many nightclubs later, they still had change in their pockets."[112] What happened in Germany was similar to what happened in China after the Second World War. Mentioned in the previous chapter was the collapse of the Chinese dollar after the war from a rate of twenty Chinese dollars to one U.S. in 1944 all the way to 1,000,000 for one in 1946. Like the German mark, the Chinese dollar gradually disappeared. Kaufman writes of how Victor Sassoon's employees "refused to take their wages in cash, insisting instead on being paid in rice, pieces of cloth, or almost anything else edible or wearable."[113]

As for modern times, in 2021 South American journalist Virginia Lopez Glass reported that "nearly 70 percent of all transactions" in Venezuela were being liquefied by U.S. dollars. Venezuela is theoretically an adversary of the U.S., but on the matter of commerce geopolitics goes out the window.[114] In 2020, Iran's monetary authorities finally replaced the rial with the toman after 3,500 devaluations of the rial since 1971,[115] but the commercial reality well before 2020 was that the "Yankee dollar" had long replaced the rial. The won is North Korea's official currency, but as the *Washington Post's* resident North Korea expert Anna Fifield reports in her 2019 book about Kim Jong-un *The Great Successor*, "Despite all the sanctions, the U.S. dollar is still the preferred currency for North Korean businessmen since it is easiest to convert and spend."[116]

Moving into March of 2022, and in the weeks after Russia's unexpected invasion of Ukraine, the Russian people got nervous. Many began to drain their U.S. dollar accounts held at Russian banks.[117] With Visa and Mastercard having subsequently suspended operations in Russia as punishment for the invasion, the *New York Times* reported on desperation among citizens "swapping intelligence on where they could still get dollars."[118] Imagine that! The dollar remains the most precious money of all in countries around the world. If money talks, the dollar talks the loudest. As Russians were moving in all directions, including out of the country altogether, access to dollars was the key to migrating successfully. For all its demerits since 1971, the dollar still reigns supreme.

Whenever a country's currency is in trouble, and in particular a currency in the Western Hemisphere, there's always talk of whether the nation in trouble will "dollarize." It's good stuff for newspapers and opinion writers, but all it really tells us is that there's confusion among government monetary authorities, and among those who report on them. In truth, dollarization is the global *rule* regardless of a country's official policy. Readers should already know why dollarization is the rule. Credible money is inevitably available where credible goods and services are being produced. Producers desire equal goods and services for the goods and services they bring to market, which means they want dollars over rubles, bolivars, tomans, and won. On this baseline, finance is lucrative. There's quite a bit of money for investment bankers and other financial types to earn for bringing producers together, and reasonably stable money is a prerequisite for trade. Producers of goods and services bring them to market to get roughly equal value back, which means producers require money that's known to hold its value.

That producers create value to get equal value naturally calls into question some common theories on inflation. Supposedly it's "too much money chasing too few goods." The characterization is lacking, and quite frankly obtuse. It implies that producers are stupid, or don't care about getting equal value such that they'll take the proverbial mark, rial, or won lying on the street before handing back real items. We know this isn't the case. While the dollar has its demerits, the fact remains that it factors into over 80 percent of international financial transactions in the present day.[119] That it does is one of those statements of the obvious demonstrated by the Asman example in St. Petersburg, but also the ones emanating from theoretically "enemy" countries like Iran, Venezuela, and North Korea. The dollar remains the currency of choice.

To then pretend that inflation is "too much money chasing too few goods" is for the definer to misunderstand how commerce works. Such a person implies with the definition that debased money is actually used by those offering goods and services for goods and services. To see why such a view is nonsense, and that by extension the definition is wanting, go back once again to the examples from Germany, China, post-Soviet Russia, Iran, North Korea, and Venezuela. The on-the-ground reality is that wrecked money doesn't play much of a role in transactions at all. "Too much money chasing too few goods" implies that producers are actively in search of ways to be ripped off. That view gets the causality backwards.

There's a popular notion that inflation is no longer a currency phenomenon born of devaluation of the unit, but instead inflation results from too much economic growth or from an economy "overheating." We can quickly put this notion to rest. For one, an economy is just people. The idea that "the Fed" or some other government entity should work to "cool" an "overheating" economy is the equivalent of Green Bay Packers head coach Matt LaFleur benching quarterback Aaron Rodgers after he throws two touchdown passes in the first quarter lest he throw two more in the second. In an economy of individuals, which is the only economy, there's no such thing as "overheating." What about "overheating" relating to labor and production capacity? Think back to the Burj Khalifa. Like anything in the world, it's a consequence of global production, and global labor. The idea of economic "slack" and other absurdities dreamt up by economists presumes that countries are impregnable islands of economic activity, as opposed to integrated parts of global wholes. Furthermore, there's the basic truth that real economic growth is instigated by investment (think savings) and the investment is inspired by an idea to produce more and more goods and services for less and less. In other words, the surest sign of a booming economy is falling prices for all manner of goods that were formerly expensive. Alas, product prices don't signal inflation or deflation as is—inflation is monetary in nature. Economists have tried to redefine it, and they've tied themselves in knots. They've also tried to tie inflation to government spending and budget deficits, but these will be addressed in the next chapter.

All of which brings us to what some would deem a more reasonable definition of inflation. It's popular to say that inflation is a consequence of central banks failing to match supply of money to demand for the same. Put another way, it is said inflation is too much currency in circulation relative to demand for it. No. *The view fails.* To see why, consider again gold's long history as the anchor for money. Are we to assume central banks in the U.S. and around the world expertly played croupier over decades and centuries of currency stability; essentially watching the gold price in dollars, pounds, francs, and other currencies in search of spikes that would signal over-issuance, and declines that would signal not enough "supply" of the currency in question? Should we assume that central banks would engage in "open market operations" to increase or shrink the "supply" of money to maintain a price? Such a view isn't serious. It presumes that monetary authorities of all stripes played expert currency trader one day, only to not play it the next. And beyond.

More realistically, the answer to true inflation (that is, a decline in the value of a currency) can be found in the memoirs of Nigel Lawson, Chancellor of the Exchequer under Margaret Thatcher. Lawson was Thatcher's equivalent of a Treasury secretary, and in 1987 monetary authorities for the G-6 countries gathered at the Louvre in Paris. The objective was more stability among the major currencies in concert with an arrest in the decline of the value of the dollar. The value of the greenback had been going south since the 1985 Plaza Accord, in which it was agreed that "some further orderly appreciation of the main non-dollar currencies against the dollar is desirable." Simply stated, greater currency stability was the goal of the Louvre gathering. Here's how Lawson described the implications of Louvre for Great Britain:

"My original post-Louvre policy was to secure sterling stability at a level higher than the pre-Louvre rate of some DM [deutschmark] 2.8, but with no specific parity in mind.

The markets, however, assumed that we must have had a desired parity and tried to guess what it was. Their guess was DM3 . . . As a result, the market started to do much of our stabilizing for us, selling sterling when it approached DM3 and buying sterling whenever it dipped below it."[120]

From Lawson's memoirs we can see that money is much more a *concept* than a commodity—which is the point. No one thinks about how many rulers are in existence in contemplating the length of a foot. A foot just *is*. No one considers how many clocks there are in contemplating the minute either. Money is a concept of value, and a measure of value, which is why it's long had standards attached to it. The standard is what matters, at which point inflation is nothing more than a *departure from a standard of value.*

In a German sense, its Bank Law of 1875 included a mark defined in terms of gold. Then, beginning in 1914, commitment to the standard became evermore tenuous, only for market actors to gradually lose trust in the standard. Post-war, commitment to the mark vanished altogether as a way of erasing war debts. Call it an imposition of socialism whereby the people paid dearly for government errors; there's more on this in the upcoming chapter. Moving to 1971, that year President Richard Nixon began to sever the dollar's link to gold at $35 an ounce—an explicit devaluation. What had anchored the dollar no longer would. This *was* the inflation, the departure from the standard itself.

All of this requires stress with post-WWI Germany top of mind. Brilliant and essential as Fergusson's book is, it arguably errs in its quoting of sixteenth century Polish King Sigismund who observed that "money loses its value when it has become too multiplied." Germany didn't have a problem of too many marks; rather its problem was that the mark lacked a standard altogether. This created a paradox in Germany: pressure on German monetary authorities "to go on printing" as the mark disappeared from circulation.[121] It was all pointless. Money that isn't trusted vanishes from commerce no matter how many notes are printed. In short, "excess money," or money that is "too multiplied," doesn't cause inflation as much as it is the logical consequence of inflation. Inflation creates money that "has become too multiplied."

This concept cannot be stressed enough: departure from the standard (the *true* inflation) *results* in too much money, as opposed to too much money causing the inflation. It's something readers of this book ideally understand innately. Precisely because all trade is products and services for products and services, money that's not trustworthy quickly ceases to be money, while the most trusted money circulates globally and in "supply" that dwarfs that of "money" that lacks any standard or trust in the marketplace.

Evidence supporting the above claim reaches us from Switzerland. As Steve Forbes, Nathan Lewis and Elizabeth Ames point out in their 2022 book *Inflation*, Switzerland can claim a rather small population of nine million in concert with a currency in the Swiss franc that is one of the most circulated forms of money in the world. Based on "money supply" theorizing of demand relative to supply, the Swiss currency would be wrecked—but it isn't. In the words of Forbes, Lewis and Ames, "the Swiss franc has been one of the world's most reliable currencies over the past hundred years," and as a result "many people outside of Switzerland "are eager to hold assets denominated in Swiss francs," plus they're eager to exchange in francs.[122] Trusted money is everywhere there is commerce, while money that's not trusted ceases to circulate. Please keep this in mind as you read commentary from Left, Right, and center about the ability of central banks to "pump" money into the economy, about them enabling growth of government via the proverbial printing press, and about their ability to fund a welfare state in total. Central banks can do no such thing. The money that actually circulates is a market phenomenon born of people and production, not a consequence of active central bankers. This will be discussed in the next chapter, as will the notion of "rising prices" as the alleged cause of inflation.

CHAPTER SEVEN

INFLATION IS NOT NECESSARILY RISING PRICES, NOR IS DEFLATION FALLING PRICES

"You can't have both your allowance and the comic book."
– Matthew Hennessey, *Visible Hand: A Wealth of Notions on the Miracle of the Market*

In 1995, tuition at Yale University was $21,000.[123] The cost (room & board were extra) was gargantuan at the time, but nowadays parents, prospective students, or both would view $21,000 as a great bargain. It's increasingly true that K-12 schooling costs well over $21,000 a year. A visit to Yale's website in 2022 indicates that tuition is $62,500, followed by room and board that push the annual number past $80,000.

There's a popular explanation among members of the political Right in the U.S. regarding soaring tuition costs. It's big government, don't you know? The previous question reads as flippant, and its tone must seem odd in a book dripping with government skepticism. No doubt, the author thinks government the incompetent barrier to progress, but every viewpoint requires careful examination. Harmful as government is, it can't be blamed for everything. It's hard to find a strong correlation between increasingly generous federal student loans and tuition. This isn't to defend those loans, even for a second.

Indeed, the deeply held view is that generous lending from the federal government devalues college degrees. Before the feds made access to college universal, getting a degree was quite the accomplishment. As a result, it mattered less where the degree came from; just getting through college academically and *financially* meant something. "I worked my way through college" opened doors for young people who didn't have family ties to the Harvards and Yales of the world and lacked real-world connections after graduation. The hard knocks quality of the whole process was the signaling device. But with the federal government playing financier of university education, what used to be a bumpy road for those lacking connections and rich parents has been smoothed. The sacrifice has been devalued, to the point that lots of people carry around degrees robbed of their essential meaning. Put another way, college was never really about the learning; it was about obtaining something challenging to get.

Still, the matter of skyrocketing tuition remains unanswered. Suggestions that soaring college costs are a consequence of federal largesse sound compelling. Why wouldn't tuition be on the way up as government steps in to foot the bill? On its face, it makes sense; but as for the tuition situation in high schools across the U.S., and where there are no (for now, at least) federal loans? Those tuition costs haven't remained flat—quite the opposite.

Take Loyola High in Los Angeles. Arguably the most prominent Catholic high school in southern California, Loyola attracts students from all points inside and well outside Los Angeles. Tuition for Loyola in 1988 was in the $2,500 per year range, while today it's a little bit north of $22,000 annually. Flintridge Preparatory School is based in La Canada-Flintridge, a town next to Pasadena, CA. While tuition in the 1980s was in the $5,000 range, nowadays the annual cost is just a little bit above $39,000. (Full disclosure: I attended both high schools). Imagine that—a private high school outside Los Angeles can now claim tuition that nearly doubles that of Yale in 1995. Another example, Harvard-Westlake High School, is on the "wrong side" of Mulholland Drive owing to its location in the San Fernando Valley. Though over the hill from the "right side" of Mulholland, more than a few children of Beverly Hills, Bel-Air and Brentwood (the "right side") attend Harvard-Westlake. Most would agree that it's the most prestigious high school in all of California. In the second half of the 1990s, tuition there was roughly $17,000. In 2022, the number has soared to $44,500 annually; a near-tripling over twenty-five years.

To all this, some readers will understandably and properly reply that anecdotes are not statistics. Three private high schools in the Los Angeles area can't necessarily be used to make a broader, national point. It's very true, but the challenge for anyone reading this is to produce information from elsewhere in the U.S. that disproves the point. In particular, they'd have to find private schools with headline tuition rates *not* noticeably different today relative to the 1980s and 1990s. The speculation is that they'd have a difficult time.

The main thing is that rising tuitions for private high schools easily disprove the popular view among economic and political pundits that rapidly growing college education costs are a direct consequence of easy federal lending. This view, as previously mentioned, is appealing at first glance. But at second glance, particularly one that includes a look at private high school tuition costs in the U.S., it's easy to see that the opinion is rather simplistic. What's the catalyst for soaring tuition costs on the high school, college, and even elementary school levels? The view here is that scarcity has combined with booming economic growth. More people have the means to purchase the items, experiences and privileges seen as elite. At the same time, you can't multiply a Loyola, a Flintridge, or any other institution.

You also can't multiply what's viewed as elite on the collegiate level. In 2022, a record 61,220 prospective students applied to Harvard, and only 1,954 were offered admission. A record 50,649 applied to Brown, and 2,546 received the proverbial fat envelope. Yale received 50,015 applications, while saying yes to only 2,234. UCLA's record application haul was 300 shy of 150,000, and 10,000 more than in 2021.[124] This is especially interesting when it's remembered that demand for leafy, majestic U.S. universities is global. While major parts of the world lived under communism or socialism in the 1980s, by the 2020s a much greater share of the world is economically free. Much more global wealth is chasing something that cannot be multiplied. In *Gaining Currency*, Eswar Prasad notes that as of 2014-15, 305,000 Chinese students lacking access to federal loans stateside were enrolled in U.S. universities, paying full tuition.[125] Once desperately poor South Korea is now intensely prosperous—so much so that 250,000 of its college-aged attend university in countries like the U.S.[126] Here too, the students receive no federal aid, yet the checkbooks stay open.

That tuition is rising is a statement of the obvious. What's elite is somewhat fixed in supply, but those who combine elite parental finances and high marks continue to multiply. The wonder is that tuition isn't *higher* considering that demand for status is somewhat inelastic. This should cause those "shocked" by the Rick Singer college admissions scandal that ensnared so many well-to-do celebrities, including Lori Loughlin and Felicity Huffman, to rethink their surprise. Even the University of Southern California is so difficult to get into that many parents have opted for bribery. When yours truly was applying to colleges, USC was known as "University of Spoiled Children" and was very much a "safety school." Nowadays, it's on the list of any top high school senior. This is arguably a happy anecdote—soaring global prosperity has brought about soaring demand for spots at elite schools. This doesn't just elevate the reputation of Harvard, Yale, and Stanford; all manner of schools gained in the process. Everyone's getting rich, or so it seems.

There's much to critique government about on the federal level; once again, it has no place in the business of student loans. But when pundits routinely argue that college tuition has well outpaced "inflation" because of federal loans, they're making an argument that doesn't stand up to either common sense or empirical reality. So, when the very excellent members of the editorial board at the *Wall Street Journal* claim that college tuition "has soared as colleges have raised prices to soak up more government subsidies,"[127] there's cause to dispute the conventional wisdom. This chapter's opening has done just that.

The tuition example provides a useful way to discuss what is (and isn't) inflation. Figure that demand for colleges and universities in the U.S. today is the visual embodiment of "too much money chasing too few goods". Demand has well outpaced supply, and prices have soared as a result. That describes the U.S. college campus of the moment, but it's also *not* inflation—not at all.

To understand why, consider the Matthew Hennessey quote that begins this chapter. The *Wall Street Journal* deputy editorial page editor was illustrating an obvious point about tradeoffs. When we buy the comic book, we have fewer dollars for other goods and services and fewer dollars to save. In the words of the always brilliant John Stuart Mill, "the payment of increased prices for some articles would draw an unusual proportion of the money of the community into the markets for those articles and must therefore draw it away from some other class of commodities, and thus lower their prices."[128]

An increase in one item's price due to a rise in demand implies a decrease in the prices of other goods, given constant real capacity to purchase. As every purchase is a tradeoff, paying more for one item can only mean reduced capacity to purchase other items and thus, lower demand. This truth has been forgotten amid the modern inflation debate. It's often claimed that economic growth causes "inflation" because demand outstrips supply. Others place the blame squarely at government largesse. Such views miss this fundamental point.

Let's address the economic growth scenario first. How do we demand things? First, we must supply—no economic school can evade this truth. In a world defined by the *getting*, productive output to provide the means for consumption comes first. In turn, rising demand is by its very descriptor a consequence of rising supply. In the previous chapter, it was asserted that falling prices for all manner of goods and services is the surest sign of economic growth. As investment powers growth, the latter is all about boosting production of goods and services at ever lower costs. Hence, prices fall during growth periods. Is this the dreaded "deflation" of economist nightmares? For the same reason that rising tuition prices aren't inflation, the answer is no. Production that results in lower prices for formerly dear products necessarily increases the amount of money we have in our pockets, and thus expands the range of products we're able to purchase.

As for government spending increasing inflation? In a January 2022 opinion piece for the *Wall Street Journal*, former Senator Phil Gramm and his co-author Mike Solon lamented inflation "driven by excess demand," and alleged that the elevated levels of the Consumer Price Index (CPI) were the result of government spending.[129] What could they have possibly meant? Their assertion was particularly unsettling given Gramm's long association with "supply-side" thought that logically sees demand as a consequence of supply. Implicit in their commentary was that governments can reach for the proverbial *other* in pursuit of spending money, only to redistribute it. Except that government can't—all demand follows supply. *Always.* For governments to shift demand into otherwise empty hands via wealth redistribution, it's only logical that others have less "demand" as a consequence. Not only were Gramm and Solon incorrect about government spending acting as an inflation accelerant, but they also mis-defined inflation. It's a departure from a monetary standard; a decline in the unit of account, not some demand-driven concept.

But don't budget deficits cause inflation? Not quite. For background, in 1819 England's debt-to-GDP ratio reached 261 percent. Consider this number for a moment, particularly through the prism of government debt as the alleged instigator of inflation. To believe Carmen Reinhart and Kenneth Rogoff, authors of the "bible" of sorts for the debt-and-deficit-obsessed titled *This Time Is Different*, England's gargantuan debt must have signaled looming economic and currency collapse for the global power. In their analysis, countries tend to tip toward decline once their debt-to-GDP ratios cross the 100 percent threshold.[130] Yet, England's economy soared in the nineteenth century. In fact, that was the country's Golden Age. Good policies tend to have that kind of effect and England during this time pursued broadly good ones. Rather than erect barriers to foreign goods and services, the political class shrunk them. Most notably in 1846, England abolished its Corn Laws that had artificially propped up grain prices through barriers to foreign imports.

It should be said firmly that whatever one's views of government debt, its existence doesn't automatically foretell economic and currency collapse. But what about Reinhart and Rogoff, some might ask? What about the 100 percent line? Quoting the great George Gilder on the matter, "History tells us that the threat to capitalism is not debt but socialism." Rather than lay its debts on the people, Great Britain protected the pound—gold factored prominently as a definer of the currency. A focus on government debt as the catalyst for economic and currency collapse misses the point and modern U.S. history proves instructive in this regard.

In 1980, total U.S. federal debt was $900 billion. At the same time, the ten-year Treasury note yielded 11 percent. Forty years later, total U.S. debt is north of $30 trillion, but the ten-year yields 3 percent, and the 3 percent cited is well above the recent norm. In short, the cost of borrowing for the U.S. has plummeted amid soaring total debt. Treasuries pay income streams in dollars, which means if inflation had reared its ugly head over the last forty years amid gargantuan increases in federal debt, this would have shown up in a rising cost of borrowing or reduced borrowing altogether. Neither happened. While Treasury's oversight of the dollar has been far from perfect since 1980, the yield on the ten-year indicates that investor trust in the dollar has grown with increased debt.

The popular view is that budget deficits cause inflation, but such a theory presumes that investors are so dense as to buy the future payment streams of countries intent on devaluing their cash flows. When investors put their wealth to work, they at least try to get positive returns. The narrative about budget deficits causing inflation suggests that investors line up to be fleeced, which is unserious thinking at best. That's not to say that governments haven't always made good on their debt. In post-WWI Germany, the mark collapsed; sometimes governments choose socialism, but it's not a hard and fast rule. If it were, there wouldn't be much government debt to speak of. You've read it before, and you'll read it again: no one wants to get ripped off.

It's all a way of making a simple case that devaluation of the currency is a *policy choice*, and that the devaluation, itself inflation, is neither a consequence of government spending nor of borrowing. No one enters the market offering more for less or provides resources to be fleeced in return. However, various economic religions believe otherwise. More confusingly, they buy into the viewpoint that debt be run up indefinitely so long as a country has a printing press. On the political Left, this ridiculous point-of-view is called Modern Monetary Theory (MMT). Its theorists contend that "countries that issue their own currencies can never 'run out of money' the way people or businesses can."[131] Some are surely laughing as they read this, particularly those on the political Right, but they would be wise to hold their laughter a bit. Members of the supply-side and Austrian School have asserted similar ideas.

In a 2021 opinion piece for the *Wall Street Journal*, Center for Financial Stability president Lawrence Goodman claimed that since 2010, "Fed purchases of Treasury debt have funded as much as 60 to 80 percent of the entire government borrowing requirement."[132] Goodman was making a comical case that the Fed, which was created by Congress, funds the borrowing of Congress. According to this reasoning, spending can be rather unlimited so long as governments have central banks. If the Gosbank (the Soviet-era central bank) just printed enough rubles to keep the country in operation, the Soviet Union would still be around today.

Except that as readers have learned, money not trusted in the marketplace is not money. We know from David Asman's time in St. Petersburg that even the Russian people didn't trust the ruble. But it's not just the supply-siders who've bought into the notion that an arm of government can fund government. Jörg Guido Hülsmann is a German-born economist who is very much a hero of the Austrian School. Books by some of their leading lights, including Carl Menger, F. A. Hayek and Ludwig von Mises can be found well read, and in abundance everywhere the author is. Menger and Mises were particularly brilliant, and Hülsmann is seen as an expert on Mises. This raises the question of why he would utter the following:

> . . . fiat money allows the government to take out loans to an unlimited extent because fiat money by definition can be produced without limitation, without commercial limitation or technological limitation, and can be produced in whatever amount is desired.[133]

If the above is not a substitutable description of MMT thinking, then nothing is. It's also absurd. Hülsmann is saying that with paper money, government borrowing has no limits. Such a misguided view has steered modern Austrians down the odd path of believing that central banks enable government without limits; that yes, government can fund government. Of course, if true, the Soviet Union would still exist. As Margaret Thatcher said about socialism, "eventually you run out of other people's money." Better yet, Mises himself was explicit in *The Theory of Money and Credit* that people "borrow money for what it can be exchanged for." It's a statement of the obvious, yet arguably Mises's foremost modern disciple presumes that the only limiting factor for government is a slow printing press.

While governments largely have a monopoly on money in modern times, markets always and everywhere render their verdicts. If markets don't trust the money brought to market, there's no debt or spending to speak of. Such is the state of things in the real world not populated by fabulist MMT proponents on the Left, supply-side happy talkers somewhere on the ideological spectrum, and increasingly conspiratorial Austrians on the Right.

In the actual world of debt, central banks can at best reflect the message of the market. The Fed can buy Treasury debt because there's huge demand for Treasuries around the world. Better yet, Treasuries are backed by the American people, who are the most productive people on earth. The Fed doesn't enable U.S. borrowing as much as the Fed can buy debt because it's a part of a government backed by the world's most productive population. Individuals like Goodman are reversing causality.

As for Hülsmann and MMT theorists like Stephanie Kelton, their theorizing presumes debt as far as the eye can see so long as a country has a paper currency. But as Eswar Prasad notes in *Gaining Currency*, "more than four-fifths of outstanding international bonds and notes" pay out dollars and euros.[134] Translated, we note that Argentina's government borrows dollars when it issues debt, as opposed to it borrowing the local, and endlessly wrecked, peso. What this tells us is that untrustworthy paper money limits government, another statement of the obvious. The implication of these findings is best summarized as follows: most governments have central banks, but most of their debt is issued in currencies other than their own.

Readers who've gotten this far know why: no one buys, sells, lends, borrows, or buys or sells shares with or for money. Money signals the flow of real resources—as such, only reasonably trusted money circulates. Some MMT and Austrian theorists would have us believe that markets are stupid, when in fact they're quite smart. Since no one wants to be ripped off, only credible currencies circulate. Since only they circulate, the ability of governments to borrow real money is limited yet again by the productivity of their people, not the idiocy of central banks armed with printers.

In other words, MMT, Austrian, and supply-side theories involving debt and inflation presume a market for debt that doesn't exist. Real investors will take dollars, euros, and similar reasonably trustworthy currencies. As a result, there's little opportunity for governments to take out loans beyond their means. If they're taking on debt, they must borrow in money that investors don't expect to be devalued, which entails a greater cost. Dollars aren't cheap to borrow.

All of which brings us to this book's penultimate chapter. It will address the 2022 inflation that arguably wasn't. Yes, you read that right. The dollar's global use as the foremost medium of exchange and debt helps make this case.

CHAPTER EIGHT

IN 2022, THEY ALL PUT ON THEIR "WIN" BUTTONS

*"The same quantity of money, besides, cannot
long remain in any country in which the value
of the annual produce diminishes."*
– Adam Smith, *The Wealth of Nations*

Gerald Ford entered the White House as President
Richard Nixon's replacement on August 9, 1974. If
Americans were expecting a better grasp of inflation from Ford
relative to his predecessor, they would soon be disappointed.

Notable about Ford's swearing in as president was that
it occurred almost exactly three years after Nixon had made
his fateful decision to sever the dollar's link to gold. It will

be stressed again that Nixon's *departure* from the standard of the dollar pegged to gold at $35 an ounce quite literally *was* the inflation. Nixon's exit from the commodity definition set in motion a sickening decline in the dollar's value. While the average price of gold in 1971 was $41 an ounce (a sign that markets had begun pricing in Nixon's errant policy choice before he made it official), by 1974 it had risen to $154. Please consider this surge in light of previous chapters' quotes from John Stuart Mill and David Ricardo. Gold is the commodity least influenced by everything else. Its constancy is what makes it useful as a definer of money, and that's why global producers happened on gold as money par excellence. But in 1971, the dollar no longer had an anchor. What occurred next was, and is, a reminder that markets always have the final say.

Though gold doesn't move, its price in terms of other currencies most certainly does. That the average price of gold nearly quadrupled from 1971 to 1974 was a flashing signal of how much the value of the dollar had declined. A dollar that had formerly been exchangeable for 1/35th of a gold ounce (or 1/41st to be precise) was now exchangeable for 1/154th of a gold ounce upon Ford's arrival at 1600 Pennsylvania Avenue. *This* was inflation. A departure from the dollar peg at $35 an ounce was an explicit devaluation that markets took seriously.

In contemplating the dollar's shrinkage relative to the constant of gold, it's useful to consider the latter versus the "rising prices" that some call inflation. They're mistaking causality when they claim rising tuition is most certainly the cause of inflation. To claim that rising prices cause inflation is like saying destroyed houses and trailers cause tornados. Causality is reversed, and at the very least confused. No doubt higher prices *can be* indicative of inflation, but as readers have hopefully concluded by now, nosebleed tuition costs have little to do with inflation. If anything, soaring tuition is a sign of a lack of inflation, considering the extent to which debased money hinders investment and thus, economic growth. Rising tuition springs from soaring global growth—that is, a lack of inflation.

Still, it's no reach to say that inflation correctly defined—a departure from a standard, a devaluation—will ultimately bring rising prices. Crucially, rising prices can be the result of inflation as opposed to its instigator. That currency devaluation would occur in concert with rising prices is one of those blinding glimpses of the obvious that rates mention. Figure that money is a veil. Fiddling with its value doesn't cause markets to stop speaking. Money is a way to measure the cost of market goods relative to one another, so it's only logical that a shrinkage of the measure would bring on higher prices. In a length or height sense, surely we could cut the foot in half so that most men would be over ten feet tall, but their actual height wouldn't change. Money's no different. Shrink it, and ultimately markets will adjust in fits and starts to the higher "money price" of goods and services.

That's what happened with President Ford. His first year in office the Consumer Price Index (CPI) registered its first ever "double digit" inflation, rising 11 percent. These indices in many ways miss the point. Rising consumer prices can be a consequence of inflation, but not always. In this case, the dollar had been devalued (real inflation), but Ford focused on the consequence of devaluation and as a result, earned his short stay in the White House. Specifically, Ford bought into the notion that rising demand was itself the inflation, while in truth, it was the falling dollar.

Armed with a definition or theory of inflation detached from reality, Ford called on Americans to, among other things, "conserve energy" to theoretically push its price down. Markets didn't comply. With an eye on bringing "balance and vitality to our economy", Ford called on every American to become an "inflation fighter", and the fight against inflation would allegedly be won if Americans mobilized for war by consuming less. Then, in October of 1974, Ford made his request of the American people programmatic, by rolling out his "Whip Inflation Now" program with its infamous WIN buttons adorning staffers in the White House.[135] You can't make this up!

What staggers the mind about then, and now too, is the willful blindness to the true nature of inflation. Soaring demand can't cause it, simply because we necessarily can't have the proverbial Yale education *and* the brand-new car or comic book or name your consumer good. In the real world, there are tradeoffs. To purchase one item is to not purchase another. If consumer demand for one item outpaces supply such that prices for that item rise, such a scenario logically implies falling prices elsewhere. It's amazing this case requires stating, but it plainly wasn't made successfully in the Ford White House of 1974. With the dollar in freefall, Ford vainly attempted to fight inflation by attacking consumerism. It's the equivalent of a patient reaching the doctor's office with a broken foot, only for the doctor to put a cast on the patient's arm. In ignoring the devaluation of the dollar, Ford's policy reaction was the ultimate *non sequitur*.

Sadly, the year 2022 revealed similarly obtuse responses to rising prices. The difference, however, is that the dollar was in freefall in 1974. In 2021-2022, it wasn't.

Regarding where we're going in this chapter, we expect readers to have some familiarity with what happened in March of 2020. That was the month that politicians on the local, state, and national levels began calling for lockdowns to slow the spread of COVID-19, a respiratory virus with origins in China. The lockdowns resulted in double digit rates of unemployment in the U.S., and literally hundreds of millions facing starvation around the world.[136] Historians will marvel at the abject stupidity of governments, and "experts" within governments. Until 2020, economic growth had always been the most formidable foe of death, disease, and sickness precisely because it produced the food people need, and the critical resources scientists use in search of cures. In 2020, politicians actively chose economic desperation as a virus mitigation strategy with no regard for knock-on effects. It truly boggles the mind.

It's useful to think of the lockdowns through the prism of one of our early case studies, the Burj Khalifa. The Burj could never have been built absent myriad inputs from around the world that made affordable a building that would be impossibly expensive to erect absent the interconnectedness of producers worldwide. Yet suddenly the interconnections were eviscerated to varying degrees. To use one of countless examples, Bangladesh has become the "sewing machine" of clothing designers the world over in modern times, yet clothing shops were closed to varying degrees due to the lockdowns. The developed world took a break from reality, and in doing so, brought on immense hardship and starvation for the people in the parts of the world doing the "dirty work" of production. Simply put, the rich U.S. designs brilliant market goods (look back to the Apple iPhone in Chapter One) and services that are manufactured elsewhere. The symmetry is quite amazing.

Then came the lockdowns; then the imposition of command-and-control such that these globalized arrangements were blown up to varying degrees from March of 2020 onward. All of which requires a pause. Consider the price implications of politicians fire-bombing business connections built up over many decades among billions of workers engaged in trillions of different commercial relationships. In an instant, they were all gone—by force. So much of the world, and most notably the developed world that is an engine for global economic activity, was no longer active. Force, by its very nature, is brutal and destructive. Unfortunately, in 2021 and 2022, the pundit class ignored the effects of such force and instead focused on prices.

Which brings us to a largely post-lockdown world that began to emerge in 2021 and included the swearing in of Joe Biden as the 46th President of the United States. Policy wise, this meant calls for a further $1.9 trillion in federal relief following the $2.9 trillion passed under President Trump. Let's be clear that this spending was yet another *non sequitur*. Americans hadn't been in desperate economic shape before the lockdowns, which means that the only reasonable economic solution was to end what had brought on the misery to begin with. Instead, with bipartisan support for massive spending plans, government proceeded to redistribute trillions in wealth, thus setting back the economy's recovery. To believe otherwise—to believe that wealth redistribution would boost economic activity—is the equivalent of saying the economy would boom if Americans started stealing from one another daily, only to go out and spend the money stolen. Of course, as any reasonably in-touch person would observe, if we all became skilled pickpockets, those robbed would have less to spend. Talent matched with capital is the only way to boost economic growth, not redistribution. In other words, a lack of spending is the only true economic "stimulus," yet the pundit class happened on the spending as the source of "demand." It was an errant analysis. With redistribution there's no increased production, which means there's no increased demand.

This is a digression in a sense. To see why, consider the eventual reaction of policy types to these redistributionist programs. Rather than point out the obvious—that they were unnecessary, and worse, that they subsidized the very lockdowns that created the desperation in the first place—the policy grandees became obsessed with "inflation." And in becoming obsessed with inflation, they redefined it. The redefinition was bipartisan.

Larry Summers, former Treasury secretary under Bill Clinton and arguably the most eminent economic theorist on the Left today, wrote in a February of 2021 opinion piece for the *Washington Post* that he feared an "overheated economy" if Biden's $1.9 trillion virus spending plan were passed. Summers's view was that the trillions would "set off inflationary pressures" from all the new consumer spending brought on by the government largesse.[137] Put another way, Summers expressed skepticism of Biden's expansive spending visions for the wrong reasons. He feared the impossibility of what some refer to as "excess demand" from the spending on the way to rising prices, but such a fear isn't rooted in reality. As has been repeated over and over, demand is a consequence of supply. To the extent that some Americans would suddenly find more money in their pockets to spend, simple logic dictates fewer dollars in the pockets of others.

Where it becomes disappointing is that Biden's critics on the Right were no better. In truth, they parroted Summers. In the world imagined by Summers *and* members of the Right, wealth would be redistributed, but those from whom wealth was redistributed wouldn't see any coincident reduction in their wealth. In a December of 2021 letter-to-the-editor published in the *Wall Street Journal,* Milton Friedman disciple Dan Thornton (former Vice President of the St. Louis Fed) asserted that all the government spending in response to lockdowns "was the equivalent of a helicopter money drop," and that "most economists believe that a very large helicopter money drop would produce inflation."[138] "Most economists," it seems, aren't in possession of much common sense.

While Summers, Thornton, Phil Gramm, and Mike Solon, and even the *Wall Street Journal*'s editorial page were explaining higher prices in 2021 and beyond as a consequence of "excess demand," their bipartisan comity was not logical. Again, it implied that consumption in the economy could be increased via wealth redistribution, which is the same as saying that thieving could bring on a Keynesian multiplier whereby the net effect of every dollar of government spending would be greater than a dollar. More realistically, the impact of government spending is by its very name negative. Figure that entrepreneurs can't innovate without capital, at which point we must consider government waste in terms of all the commercial ideas and businesses that never happen as politicians consume precious resources.

After which, it cannot be stressed enough that the act of saving in no way shrinks demand as is. As discussed at this book's front, what's unspent is shifted to others in market-driven fashion. Money isn't warehoused; rather what's unspent is shifted to ever higher uses. The level of "demand" in the economy that Left and Right said was causing inflation would have been there no matter what. Even the great Judy Shelton, a longtime free market stalwart, claimed in the *Wall Street Journal* that with CPI inflation at a forty-year high, a "major cause" was "the federal government's putting additional money in the hands of consumers, increasing demand, without increasing supply."[139] Shelton most certainly knows better. Supply and demand mirror one another.

In the policy scrum of 2021 and 2022, high-end policy theorists on both sides unwittingly donned the "WIN" pins that properly made Gerald Ford a laughingstock in the 1970s. Paraphrasing Ford's former boss, *they were all demand-siders.* The main thing is that while misguided on too many levels to count, the government spending that President Biden wanted (but thankfully didn't get in total) had no inflationary qualities. Inflation is a policy choice of currency devaluation, it's a departure from what makes money *money.* Nothing else.

Other self-styled inflation hawks pointed to the Federal Reserve. Despite the dollar's exchange value not being part of the Fed's portfolio as is (more on this in the concluding chapter), economists like John Greenwood and Steve Hanke pointed to the Fed's growing "balance sheet" that was built by "large-scale asset purchases." The Fed would purchase low-risk Treasuries and other interest-bearing debt from financial institutions. At the same time, risk-averse banks held growing amounts of their reserves at the Fed, and the Fed paid them low levels of interest on the funds. There's your "balance sheet" increase that supposedly was creating trillions "of new money in the system" and allegedly pushing up inflation.[140] Except that it wasn't, nor is there much of a story here. Banks, as readers know, are risk averse. Their aversion led them to keep funds with the central bank, only for the Fed to put the funds to work. In purchasing low-risk assets, the Fed was buying what other money sources would have purchased.

In another opinion piece for the *Wall Street Journal* a month later, Greenwood and Hanke called for the Fed to plan "a 'golden growth' rate of around 6%" for the so-called "money supply."[141] But the Fed can do no such thing. As the Adam Smith quote that begins this chapter correctly points out, real money that facilitates exchange is naturally abundant where production is abundant, and it's naturally scarce where production is scarce. Greenwood and Hanke would have us believe that a market phenomenon born of production should actually be planned by governments. This has long been the belief of "monetarists," including their modern patriarch, the late Nobel Laureate Milton Friedman.

In Friedman's own words, "government must provide a monetary framework for a competitive order since the competitive order cannot provide one for itself."[142] Friedman was plainly brilliant—so brilliant that it's not the author's place to describe him as such. Still, on the matter of money he got things exactly backwards. All production is an expression of demand for other goods and services, after which money is yet again a natural occurrence of the marketplace; an occurrence as natural as production itself. Yet Friedman was of the view that this natural market function should be planned by monetary philosophers in the employ of government. The very notion that central banks could plan so-called "money supply," or, per Greenwood and Hanke some kind of "golden growth" rate just spoke to how backwards the monetary discussion had become in 2021-2022.

Most disappointing was the migration of the *Wall Street Journal's* editorial page toward monetarist orthodoxy whereby a market concept needed to be planned. In a June of 2022 opinion piece in which he commented on what he deemed rising inflation, columnist Holman Jenkins referenced the Reagan years, "and the Fed's turn toward Milton Friedman-esque monetarism."[143] An accompanying editorial on the same day as Jenkins's column claimed much the same, that the Fed's migration toward "tighter money" was "the Ronald Reagan-Paul Volcker formula that broke inflation in the 1980s and led to a boom."[144] Were he alive, Robert L. Bartley, editorial page editor of the *Wall Street Journal* during the Reagan years, would have corrected what was so confidently stated. Though he thought a great deal of Volcker, Bartley was taught monetary policy by Robert Mundell, and Mundell was the one who quipped "the only closed economy is the world economy." The late Mundell knew well, like Arthur Laffer, that so-called "money supply" was "demand determined," as in it was a consequence of production.[145] By extension, Bartley knew all this.

Bartley wrote a wonderful book on the Reagan years (*The Seven Fat Years*) in which he was clear that while Milton

Friedman was "entirely at home" with Laffer, Mundell, Jude Wanniski, Bartley himself, and countless other Reagan-era economic thinkers on most matters economic, he wasn't in agreement with the Reagan crowd "on his centerpiece, controlling 'the money supply.'"[146] It cannot be stressed enough that Friedman's views on money were decidedly not those of Laffer, Mundell, Bartley, and Reagan himself. While Friedman promoted the statist fallacy of centrally planned "money supply" without regard to commodity definitions, Reagan ran on reviving the dollar with exactly that. In his words, "No nation in history has ever survived fiat money, money that did not have a precious metal backing."[147] And while Reagan never succeeded in re-linking the dollar to gold, we know from Chapter Six and Nigel Lawson's recall of the market's reaction to his desire for a British pound price rule that markets respond to words. To some degree Reagan got the dollar he wanted, and so-called "money supply" had nothing to do with it. Notable about all this is that Friedman became a skeptic of the Reagan policy mix.

In 1983, when the U.S. economy started to take off, Friedman declared that "double digit" inflation was inevitable thanks to growth in various monetary aggregates. And then when he detected what he considered a slowdown in monetary growth in late 1983, he predicted a recession that would harm Reagan in his re-election year.[148] Actually, the economy boomed and Reagan won by a landslide, 49 states to one (Minnesota). When Volcker's initial term came up as Fed Chairman, Reagan didn't even want to re-appoint him.[149] All of this is hopefully a useful digression for revealing how the monetarist approach to money was *not* part of the Reagan economic revival as the most important editorial page in the world (the *Wall Street Journal's*) claims now. Crucially, this isn't some idle assertion. It's all well-documented in the masterful book by the editor of the *Journal's* editorial page during the Reagan years.

Furthermore, the focus on the "money supply" gets things backwards. Those who buy into it presume that rising money in circulation is inflationary, while "tight" money such that it's limited in "supply" is the path to nirvana. More realistically, good money is the most circulated of all. If you're scratching your head, look back to Chapter Six and the brief discussion of the Swiss franc. Precisely because the franc is so trusted, it's one of the most circulated currencies in the world. Conversely, in the same chapter we see how the toman in Iran, the won in North Korea, and the bolivar have been replaced by the dollar in all three countries despite their "enemy" status.

Please consider this alongside all the monetarist alarmism of 2021 and 2022. Supposedly good times could be had if the allegedly inflationary dollar's supply were managed by wise central bankers; but the dollar liquefies something on the order of 70 percent of transactions in Venezuela, it along with the euro is the currency paid out in nearly all forms of global debt, not to mention that per Eswar Prasad's 2021 book, *The Future of Money*, "more than half of all U.S. currency is held abroad," while 24 percent of total currency in circulation globally is in dollars.[150] If the dollar were as weak as the monetarists presume, this would show up in circulation. What's in decline is logically circulated less because—you've read it before—producers don't want to get ripped off.

After which, money goes where it's going to be treated well: where commerce is abundant. That the dollar circulates in the U.S. while also moonlighting as the world's currency is a sign that "money supply" isn't planned by central bankers—its movements could never be planned. Such a notion is as fork-in-the-eye foolish as the Soviet Union's Five-Year Plans of the past. Since economic activity can't be decreed, neither can the money quantity necessary to move production ever higher.

To be clear, the dollar's global circulation is not a full-throated endorsement of U.S. dollar policy. As evidenced by the proliferation of currency trading since the 1970s, the dollar's instability has sadly created a new industry of facilitators over producers as wise minds have begun trading currencies for a living; they do God's work. We must make sense of the chaos wrought by unstable money. At the same time, it should be said that the dollar's role as the near-constant measure facilitating trade signals that, as money goes, it's the most trusted currency of them all. In which case, it's useful to imagine what would happen if the dollar once again had a stable, commodity definition. If so, it's not unrealistic to say that dollars would facilitate even more global exchange and investment, only for supply of the currency to skyrocket? Monetarists would yell "inflation," but the reality would be quite different. Contra monetarists, there can never be too much money any more than there could never be too much production.

The main thing is that monetary stability would free countless wonderful minds from facilitator roles such as traders and propel them into production and the financing of production. The latter would create stunning global growth with money once again filling its singular role as a measure fostering the movement of goods, services, and labor to their highest uses. Under such a scenario, money in circulation would soar as a natural consequence of soaring production. As always, money doesn't instigate. Money is the consequence.

Still, there's the matter of rising prices in 2021 and 2022. To deny that a variety of prices soared during the timeframe in question would amount to willful blindness. The quibble here is not with rising prices, but whether they were evidence of inflation. It will all begin with "They just thank me profusely, so much that I'm like, 'Oh, my God,' I was literally only here for three hours." The quoted person is Dani Gantcher, an eighteen-year old living in Scarsdale, New York. She was featured in a 2022 *Wall Street Journal* front page story about the rising hourly wages enjoyed by babysitters. The report indicated much better pay, greatly reduced expectations and chores, plus better snacks.[151]

The word on the street post-lockdown was that parents in greater numbers needed babysitting help. It was work, but surely for others it was a desire to be out and about again. Call it a mad rush among married couples for "date nights."

About this, some reading this paragraph are wondering who would let a virus keep them homebound. The author shares your wonderment, but our bemusement is not the point. Amid a big surge in demand for babysitting, the price of securing the service rose.

So did demand for cars increase, for Uber drivers in those cars, for lumber to build houses. Love or hate the lockdowns, and I hate them, what's undeniable is that a year or two of relatively empty freeways, streets, and skies arguably warped the wants and needs of those who had been shut in either by choice or by force. Goodness, even a movie theater popcorn shortage revealed itself in June of 2022.[152]

You quite simply can't take away freedom in the way that politicians did, and not expect demand and supply mismatches in the aftermath. About this, let's be clear that supply is the mirror image of demand. That hasn't changed. But in any market economy consumer preferences change all the time. To offer but one of countless examples, a *Forbes* magazine cover in 2007 featured Nokia and its ubiquitous mobile phone, along with the question, "Can Anyone Catch the Cell Phone King?"[153] Applied to the post-lockdown world, supply of certain goods wasn't ready for changed demand, so prices rose to reflect this reality. Inflation? Obviously not. When consumers bid one item or many items up, other prices logically fall.

From there, it's useful to pivot to the risks businesses faced post-lockdown; in particular, the risks related to further takings of freedom. Though he wasn't writing about lockdowns in his 2022 book *Visible Hand,* deputy editorial page editor at the *Wall Street Journal* Matthew Hennessey wrote of the difficulties of running a restaurant. This was a business with which he was familiar, given his late parents' ownership of a popular bar/restaurant in Morristown, NJ, appropriately called Hennessey's. Hennessey made the point that restaurants face the nightly worry of having too much or too little inventory. Maybe the owner buys a limited number of hamburgers and buns for a normally slow Monday evening, only for a couple of softball teams to show up postgame. The fear of the unknown naturally requires restaurants to hold extra inventory to be ready for an unexpected rush, but if it doesn't materialize, the inventory must be thrown out. The cost of carrying inventory that will eventually be tossed factors into the prices we pay for all manner of goods and services.

Thinking about all this through the prism of the postlockdown environment, is it any surprise that prices are higher in consideration of what took place in 2020? The U.S. economy was booming, then it was shuttered. To then pretend that business owners of all stripes wouldn't charge higher prices with the risk of future shutdowns top of mind is just naïve. Inflation? No, just businesses bending to reality.

What about simple access to market goods in the aftermath of lockdowns? It's a useful question in consideration of the global economy in which we're operating. In a December 2021 interview in the *Wall Street Journal,* Flexport (a global shipping logistics company) chief economist Phil

Levy noted that while the pre-virus shipment of a container from China to the U.S. took 71 days, the post-virus number is up to 117. Much worse is the cost. While it might have cost $1,500 pre-virus to get a container across the Pacific Ocean, post-virus prices were more in the $15,000 range. Perhaps most useful here is what the shipping costs have meant for lower-value goods. In the interview he made the point that a container of relatively cheap goods worth $15,000 could be reasonably shipped at prices of $1,500, but at $15,000?[154] Thinking about airlines, they went from full planes to empty planes and furloughed employees. As airports and planes started to fill up, it's only logical that cancellations rose too. It's difficult to quickly re-staff what had been shuttered, plus it's risky. Pathogens are a part of life. How to re-staff with the possibility of further shutdowns looming? And what of the employees of airlines, restaurants and countless other commercial entities?

What are they to do? Just come back at the old pay? Some would ask why come back at all to businesses so easily shuttered by nail-biting politicians, which is a worthy question. Post-lockdown there was a "Great Resignation" and "labor shortage" narrative that in some ways ignored the greater truth that humans are the ultimate form of capital, and the cost of winning their services would have to rise to reflect the risks inherent in accepting a job or keeping one that could so easily vanish. Lest readers forget, a quarter of the U.S. workforce was rendered jobless by the lockdowns. Based on that, wouldn't it be logical for those made unemployed to approach future work more skeptically? And with more demands. Except that this is not inflation. This was, and is, the warping of price signals by politicians.

It's also possible that a variety of virus-related unemployment benefits just added to the ease with which workers stayed sidelined. The view here is that this is overstated, but it's surely debatable. What's not debatable is that the benefits boosted "demand" in the economy, thus driving up prices. It didn't; demand was shifted.

This brings us to a discussion earlier in this chapter: the remarkably global nature of everything. As noted in Chapter One, Hillary Clinton was wrong about it "taking a village." When it comes to production, in modern times it takes the world. Think of the Burj yet again. Absent remarkable advances achieved around the world in the creation of concrete, the transportation of concrete to ever higher levels in rapid fashion, and endless other tiny in size but essential consequences of uniquely specialized work, there's no remotely affordable way to build the world's tallest building. Going back even further in time, consider the pin factory that Adam Smith witnessed in the eighteenth century. One man working alone could maybe produce one pin per day, but one man working with several others could produce tens of thousands. Work divided is the path to lower and lower prices simply because the more that work is divided up among the specialized around the world, the exponentially greater output can be produced.

The above is simple to understand, but notably lacking in the popular discourse as of this book's writing. It demands deep thought in consideration of what politicians did to global "supply chains" in 2020. "Supply chains" are put in quotes as they're not tangible objects. In truth, they are once again the result of billions of workers engaged in trillions of increasingly sophisticated commercial relationships, working together in a symmetry that brings new meaning to the word remarkable. Quite simply, everything that's produced is born of staggeringly sophisticated cooperation among individuals, machines, engineers, operations, and management experts the world over. And then, once again, the lockdowns.

What vandalized common sense and eviscerated processes operating in precision-like fashion rendered the world unemployed to various degrees. Workers were displaced globally much as they were stateside, only for politicians to gradually return to the locked down their former freedoms. Of course, during that time consumer habits had changed (or had been warped), financial situations had been changed for the good and better; and those forced out of work entered a different world, one that had changed them as much as it had changed. The people are the global economy and the people emerged from lockdowns with understandably different views of work, including about the jobs they once had. Just as there was mass turnover stateside, does anyone think humanity is much different elsewhere?

Yet politicians expected prices to remain the same. So did economists. So did pundits. The arrogant foolishness of such an assumption made Barack Obama's "You didn't build that" line seem polite by comparison. Politicians did great damage to the global miracle of production that prevailed before the lockdowns, only to expect the miracle to revive itself, fully intact, once freedoms taken were gradually returned in patronizing fashion. Life doesn't work that way, but to economists, politicians, and experts it seemed as if it should. The political, pundit, and expert classes, entirely unharmed by the lockdowns, continued to pursue *non sequiturs*. Most obnoxiously, former Federal Reserve vice chairman Kevin Warsh penned a *Wall Street Journal* opinion piece in which he arrogantly dismissed "supply-chain bottlenecks" as the source of rising prices based on the assertion that "prices are rising at the points of production, assembly and transportation."[155] To Warsh, it had to be the Fed as inflation's instigator. Without defending the Fed for even a second, what did the central bank have to do with the lockdowns? For Warsh to dismiss the price implications of supply-chain impairment, impairment that would logically and painfully be felt at all points of production, was awe-inspiring for its tone deafness, but more shocking in the economic ignorance that it conveyed. It's also interesting to note that when the lockdowns began, Warsh was publishing op-eds in the *Journal* proposing Federal Reserve "liquidity" programs whereby the central bank would direct funds to businesses being suffocated by the lapse of reason. A truly helpful op-ed would have acknowledged that liquidity is always and everywhere the *consequence* of businesses operating free of command-and-control, at which point Warsh should have called for an end to the lockdowns. Alas, the Fed and other policy actions for those on the inside are the all-weather solutions to everything. Freedom? Oh wow, so low rent . . .

Higher prices in the aftermath of crushing lockdowns are a statement of the obvious. They weren't caused by government spending or "money supply," but instead were the logical consequence of impairing the interconnectedness among man and machine that makes ever-falling prices a possibility in the first place. To be clear, higher prices did reveal themselves in 2021 and beyond, but as this book has made plain, there's a big difference between rising prices born of currency devaluation versus the imposition of command-and-control. The latter is not inflation.

All of which brings us closer to this chapter's close. No doubt some are asking about gasoline prices. Didn't President Biden's "war on oil" cause them to rise? It's best to answer the previous question with another question. Did former oilman George W. Bush's admiration for the industry cause oil prices to decline? Bush's presidency is germane to the discussion simply because as gasoline prices soared in 2022, it's notable that they reached levels not seen since 2008.[156] What was the price of a barrel when Bush reached the White House in 2001? A look on Google reveals roughly $25. Further digging shows a barrel could be had for $10 in 1998 during Bill Clinton's presidency, and $9 during Reagan's. Reagan's presidency is notable mainly because as *Wall Street Journal* reporter Gregory Zuckerman wrote in his 2013 book *The*

Frackers, "the 1980s were among the worst periods in the history of the domestic energy industry" during which time an "estimated 90 percent of oil and gas companies went out of business."[157] Did Reagan despise the oil industry? No, but he thought a weak dollar truly harmful to every American as has already been discussed.

It's a quick way of saying that when dollar policy favors stability and strength, as was the case during the presidencies of Reagan and Clinton, oil is nominally cheap; so cheap that domestic production is a non-starter. Indeed, as Zuckerman reported about drilling in fracking-rich North Dakota, costs of extraction "in the region were so high that it didn't pay to do any drilling unless crude prices were at fifty or sixty dollars a barrel."[158] There's your answer: dollar policy is the biggest factor when it comes to the oil price, and Bush pursued a weak dollar only for the price per barrel to skyrocket on his watch. Markets respond to words more than people realize, and during Bush's presidency his first Treasury secretary in Paul O'Neill made plain that a strong dollar was not a priority, while his second, John Snow, asked at 2007 meeting of the G-8 countries "What's wrong with a weak dollar?"[159] Once again, inflation is a policy *choice*, and it's a choice the Fed is not empowered to make. This will be covered more in the concluding chapter. For now, while the average price of gold during Bush's first year in office was $271, during his final year in office the average price had more than tripled to $871. The dollar had fallen substantially. Real inflation.

Better yet, it helps to explain still nosebleed oil prices under President Biden. In short, the weak dollar fire lit by George W. Bush continued to varying degrees under Presidents Obama and Trump. Gold hit an all-time high of $1,900/ounce in 2011, and it was trading above $1,800 when Biden replaced Trump. It's a long way of saying that while rising prices were a sad consequence of lockdowns, the devaluation of the dollar has been the norm for the 21st century. The inflation wasn't Biden's alone. This isn't a defense of him; it's just an acknowledgement that as of this writing, the dollar price of gold is in 2022 is just slightly lower than it was in January of 2021. To be fair, the lockdowns that are the true author of rising prices began when Joe Biden was a private citizen. It's likely this most limited of thinkers would have done the same as Donald Trump did with perhaps a more draconian tinge, but counterfactuals are just that.

The 2022 inflation largely wasn't, and what was inflation was something Biden inherited. But for the nosebleed cost of everything that rightly has so many so very much on edge, command-and-control is decidedly not inflation.

All of which brings us to the book's conclusion. It's an optimistic one about the future of money and, in turn, of the future itself.

THE INEVITABILITY OF CRYPTO

"Most people think money has power in and of itself. But actually, it's really just an information system, so that we don't have to engage in barter and that we can time shift value in the form of loans and equity and stuff like that."[160]
– Elon Musk

In 1933, in his first year in office, President Franklin Delano Roosevelt made the damaging decision to devalue the dollar from a fixed rate of $20.67 per ounce of gold to $35. Carmen Reinhart and Kenneth Rogoff described FDR's action in their 2009 book *This Time Is Different* as a default. In their words, "The abrogation of the gold clause in the United States in 1933, which meant that public debts would be repaid in fiat currency rather than gold, constitutes a restricting of nearly all the government's domestic debt."[161]

Per the Elon Musk quote that begins this chapter, money is crucially an "information system." In a rational world it's the very quiet measure with foot, minute, and tablespoon-like qualities that reflects reality in terms of a unit—in our case the dollar unit. But in 1933, the dollar measure was decreased 59 percent by presidential decree. Consider the meaning of this. When investors value companies, they're speculating on all the dollars such a company will ever earn. Imagine what devaluation does to investor projections, and to contracts and wages amongst other things. There are no companies and no jobs without investment first and when investors put wealth to work, they're seeking returns in dollars. Imagine what FDR's decision meant for them. Worse, FDR reserved the right to further fiddle with the dollar's value as he saw fit. Historian Amity Shlaes described FDR's shallow thought process in her 2007 book *The Forgotten Man*:

> One morning, FDR told his group he was thinking of raising the gold price by twenty-one cents. Why that figure? His entourage asked. 'It's a lucky number,' Roosevelt said, 'because it's three times seven.' As [Treasury secretary] Morgenthau later wrote, 'If anybody knew how we really set the gold price through a combination of lucky numbers, etc., I think they would be really frightened.'[162]

You think? Imagine investing in such an environment when the dollar used to measure returns or lack thereof could be revalued at random, without regard, for any reason, and on the way to substantial shrinkage of any returns. This book is decidedly not about the Great Depression, but it's worth reiterating that the stated reason for the Fed's culpability in the long downturn (tight so-called "money supply") is so divorced from reality as to make those of sound mind seriously question the intelligence of the self-styled policy elite. The Fed's well overstated role in the 1930s has already been discussed.

Still, the Fed rates further mention in terms of FDR's mindless devaluation of the dollar to make a broader point. So horrified was Federal Reserve Chairman Eugene Meyer by FDR's decision, that he resigned. Not long after, Meyer purchased the *Washington Post* at an auction, only to hire an editor (Ralph Robey) with whom he would work to "fight the inflationary policies of Mr. Roosevelt and his crowd."[163] Notable about Meyer's resignation is that while he was very much opposed to FDR's devaluation, Shlaes writes that "It did not matter what the Federal Reserve said."[164] No, it didn't.

Fast forward to 1971; readers already know that President Nixon decided in that year to sever the dollar's link to gold. What is less well known is Federal Reserve Chairman Arthur Burns' passionate opposition to Nixon's decision. In order to fill in these unsung blanks, we'll turn to Steven Hayward's *The Age of Reagan: The Fall of the Old Liberal Order, 1964-1980*, in which Hayward wrote that "Fed Chairman Arthur

Burns opposed the move [leaving gold], predicting that the stock market would crash and that *Pravda* would have a field day by saying the abandonment of the gold standard was a sure sign of the collapse of capitalism."[165]

In Rice University professor Allen J. Matusow's 1998 book, *Nixon's Economy*, he reported that after Nixon and his advisers made the decision about the dollar's devaluation, "Burns stayed behind to make a last plea for gold."[166] And then in *Inside the Nixon Administration: The Secret Diary of Arthur Burns, 1969-1974*, entries routinely note Burns's dismay about Nixon leaving gold, including one in which he wrote "My efforts to prevent the closing of the gold window—working through Connolly, Volcker, and Shultz—do not seem to have succeeded. The gold window may have to be closed tomorrow because we now have a government that seems incapable, not only of constructive leadership, but of any action at all. What a tragedy for mankind!"[167]

Why all this in a book that has routinely dismissed the central bank's power? The answer to the question in many ways can be found in the question. Not only are the Fed's rate machinations vis-à-vis banks not of any import to the real economy—it's worth noting that the correlation between the opening of the Fed's doors in 1913 with the dollar's 90 percent plus descent since then is spurious. Figure that the Fed had been operating for twenty years before 1933, only for the first dollar devaluation during the Federal Reserve era to occur amid vehement opposition from the Fed Chairman. What was true in 1933 was similarly true in 1971. The inflationary actions of two presidents took place despite central bank opposition.

The simple but lost-in-conspiracy-theories truth about the Fed is that the dollar's exchange value is not part of its portfolio and it never has been. This isn't a plea for sympathy regarding the Fed, as much as it's a desire to set the record straight. Inflation is always and everywhere a *policy choice*, and it's one that has historically been arrived at by presidents. Furthermore, even if it were true that the dollar's exchange rate was part of the Fed's portfolio, it would be of no consequence. Lest readers forget, the Fed is an arm of government. As this book has regularly stated, the Fed is not an *"other"* and the pretense that it's independent is laughable given the Office of the President appoints top Fed officials. The point? Governments devalue—they always have. For one to focus on the Fed while properly decrying currency devaluation is to miss the point. And it's to miss a historical truth of the last one hundred years that presidents get the dollar they want. FDR did. So did Nixon. So did Carter, Reagan, Clinton, Bush and everyone in between and beyond.

All of which brings us to two quotes: one from Adam Smith and one from John Maynard Keynes. To most reading this book, there is perhaps an expectation of opposition to the free-market Smith and the big-government promoting Keynes, but particularly with his early work, it's evident that Keynes thought quite a bit like the classical liberals including Smith, Mill and Ricardo. In Smith's case, he observed that ". . . land is a subject which cannot be removed, whereas stock easily may. The proprietor of land is necessarily a citizen of the particular country in which his estate lies. The proprietor of stock is properly a citizen of the world and is not necessarily attached to any particular country."

Writing about inflation in *A Tract on Monetary Reform*, Keynes wrote that "Its most striking consequence is its *injustice* to those who in good faith have committed themselves to titles to money rather than to things." It's worth pointing out again how much Smith and Keynes thought alike at times. Smith was a skeptic of home ownership because he well understood that consumption of housing came at the expense of the savings without which there was no progress. Smith was also making a case that mobility of human capital to its highest use was the biggest driver of capitalistic progress precisely because the most important capital of all would not be tied down by where "his estate lies." Keynes was writing of the horrors of inflation for it rewarding the individual for owning *things*, including a home, instead of titles to future wealth creation.

It's been written before in this short book that inflation is a progress retardant despite what economists near monolithically believe, and it's worth pointing out that two alleged ideological opposites in Smith and Keynes knew this to be true. Translating their genius, when devaluation rears its ugly head, the incentive is to exchange money for real things like land, housing, rare art, stamps, and commodities. Yes, the incentive is to exchange declining money for *wealth that already exists*. Conversely, when money is stable, and expected to remain stable, there's a greater willingness to direct it in intrepid fashion. With the risk of devaluation off the table, there's a greater willingness to direct it to stocks and bonds (titles) representing wealth that *doesn't yet exist*.

Which of those options drives economic progress, opportunity, jobs, health, and all sorts of other good things? Readers surely know the answer by now. And in knowing the answer, you know what fools economists have been making of themselves for decades with their troglodytic assertions about the good of currency devaluation, two percent inflation, and other mindless policy notions. Money has one purpose per Smith: to move consumable goods around, and ultimately to their highest use. As the Elon Musk quote that begins this chapter reveals, his view of money as an "information system" is the same as Smith's definition. Money is quiet as any good measure would be. It's the information conveyed through money, including rapid exchange of goods, services, and labor that gives money a purpose. Without the latter, money has no purpose.

For money to have meaning, there must be people and production. When economists talk of "gunning the money supply" and other fabulist notions, they embarrass themselves for putting the cart before the horse. Where there's people and production, there's no need to gun anything. Again, money is a natural occurrence where there's productive activity because the sole purpose of production is the *getting*. As an agreed upon measure of value, money facilitates the *getting*, but only insofar as there's already production. *Money is as natural in proper amounts as production.* You can't stimulate with devaluation, and as for "money creation," it's similarly a natural occurrence that real money departs in seconds from locales bereft of production. This is what financial intermediaries do.

Reducing the above to the absurd, imagine the Fed pumping money into banks in perpetually impoverished Cairo, Illinois. Could this stimulate anything? No—it would be irrelevant. Bank loans must perform; in the words of Ogden Nash from *Bankers Are Just Like Anybody Else, Except Richer*[168], "you must never lend any money to anybody unless they don't need it," and the people in Cairo need it, desperately. Money "gunned" or "pumped" into Cairo banks would rapidly exit Cairo, care of careful bankers. Fed attempts to shrink money in technology locales like Mountain View, California or Austin, Texas would similarly be in vain. Money goes where it's treated best—always, always, always.

Yet there remains the matter of inflation. Governments devalue, and their devaluations distort the natural act of *getting*, which is another word for trade. Again, people don't want to be ripped off, but floating money values can naturally lead to quite the opposite. This is true even with the dollar. A dollar that on average purchased roughly 1/275th of a gold ounce in 2000 purchases 1/1,850th of a gold ounce in 2022. This cannot be dismissed. The most trusted currency in the world as circulating money indicates is still not wholly reliable. And for those who still think gold an irrelevant measure, please re-read Chapter Two to see how much markets clearly view gold as an enormously *reliable* measure.

Where it gets interesting is that we can do better thanks to the very cryptocurrencies that are presently being dismissed. As this chapter is being written in June of 2022, cryptocurrencies are in freefall. As noted in this book's introduction, Bitcoin has fallen all the way to $19,000 after fetching $68,000 in November of the previous year. A *Wall Street Journal* headline confidently asserts that "The Crypto Party Is Over."[169] But in reality, the party is just beginning, and the evidence is the collapse of so many formerly high-flying currencies. They're the signal that the market for private money is real—that there's actual thought going into what was formerly defined by "Fear of Missing Out". Lest readers forget, every commercial advance is dominated by crushing failure. In the early part of the twentieth century thousands of car companies formed, only for very few to survive. In the late twentieth century the Internet was all the rage on the way to a major rush of human, physical, and financial capital out to Silicon Valley. In 2001 most of the startups went bust, but as opposed to heralding the end of the Internet boom, this necessary shakeout of the bad signaled a positive release of crucial human, physical and financial capital from poorly run companies to much better ones. Proof that mass failure doesn't end the proverbial party is how automobiles and Internet concepts define our lives in the twenty-first century.

Let's call the collapse in crypto concepts an information-producing "growth spasm" a la George Gilder. What's worthwhile, what's transformative invariably attracts copious amounts of intrepid (and yes, sometimes *stupid*) investment that produces the information necessary for progress. Without failure, including failure born of "dumb money" capital allocations, there is no progress. Where will Bitcoin, Ethereum and other prominent early arrivals to the crypto space end up? The speculation here, and that was first expressed in a June of 2021 column titled "We'll Know Crypto Is For Real When Its Coins Start Collapsing,"[170] is that the early arrivals will gradually be replaced by better known names of commerce. What will they be? The answer to the previous question can't properly be answered without first stressing what is undeniably true: ***private money forms will inevitably replace government money because they will have to***. Yes, crypto or private money is certainly the future for two reasons: because we *must* have much more trustworthy money in order to achieve our human potential, and because we *can*.

Let's start with *must*. For background, it's useful to quickly travel back in time to 1964 when IBM rolled out its first mainframe computer, the IBM System/360. If you wanted to own this most massive of contraptions that was slower than slow, and that lacked any of the features including internet that none of us could live without today, you were going to pay well over a million dollars for the most bare bones of versions.[171]

Roughly ten years before IBM's System/360 reached the markets, the world's self-proclaimed "Greatest Living Architect" in Frank Lloyd Wright held a press conference at which he talked about his vision for a 'Sky-City' with a building that would rise 528 stories into the sky, that would have landing pads for one hundred helicopters, parking spaces for 15,000 cars, and 76 "yet-to-be-invented 'atomic-powered' elevators, each capable of racing up to sixty miles per hour." Wright's vision was to reclaim massive amounts of land in major cities through cities that would soar well into the sky. But as architect and *Supertall* author Stefan Al wrote in his remarkable 2022 book, "Despite Wright's immense reputation, no one dared to think of building the project."[172] Well, of course not. But as this book's introductory chapter reveals, what was once viewed as impossible and too expensive by many, many miles, is now possible. And it's happening. The Burj is the world's tallest building at half of a mile, but it could soon be eclipsed by Saudi Arabia's Jeddah Tower, which upon completion will rise two-thirds of a mile into the sky.

There are realistically no limits to human ingenuity. As we see repeatedly, the more that work can be divided by humans, and by humans with machines, the exponentially more that we can produce at prices that continue to fall. Our specialization renders us much more productive, only for us to develop goods, services, and inputs capable of turning grandiose visions into awe-inspiring reality. It perhaps sounds trite, but our capacity for innovation is limitless so long as we're able to work together.

Money that's stable as a measure of value fosters enormous amounts of collaborative work at all points around the globe precisely because it's trusted. If the measure is consistent, we can confidently interact reasonably certain that at least in a monetary sense, none of us will get ripped off when we bring the fruits of our own labor to the marketplace. It's all something to think about in terms of the "trade wars" that have reared their ugly selves more and more since the 1970s. Is anyone surprised by this development? Floating money naturally creates winners and losers in transactions that should be mutually enhancing simply because money's worth is in the goods and services for which it can be exchanged. But what money buys on a daily-basis changes all the time in a world defined by currencies without anchor. Looked at in the extreme sense, consider yet again Bitcoin's volatility. How does one buy, sell, lend, or borrow using that which has no fixed value? Depending on which direction Bitcoin moves, those who use it as a dollar replacement will either win big or lose big. Bitcoin's present volatility surely magnifies the dollar's demerits as a not entirely trustworthy measure, but that's why Bitcoin is so important. We will learn from it.

Why can we write a much better crypto (but realistically private money) future? To see why consider the Burj, but also the smartphone that sits in your pocket, on which you perhaps ordered this book, and that maybe you're even using to read this book. In your hand is a veritable super-computer with exponentially more power and capabilities that the IBM Select/360 that cost well over $1 million. You likely bought what's much better for several hundred dollars, or maybe even less than that based on an agreement with a service provider.

What requires stress is that a capitalist system that can erect buildings that soar into the sky, and supercomputers that fit in our pockets, can surely design a monetary unit that has foot, minute, and tablespoon-like qualities. While Milton Friedman surprisingly called for "a reform of the monetary and banking system to eliminate both the private creation or destruction of money"[173] in 1948, the happy reality is that private creation of money will surely define the future. It will because as utilized as the dollar and euro have become globally, $10 trillion in daily currency trading signals that they're not trusted enough. And since they're not, the loss of economic progress born of currency risk is too great.

To this, some will say the risk is in private issuers of money. A *Wall Street Journal* editorial from May of 2022 (when the crypto correction began) noted that "While fiat currencies such as the dollar are backed by government, crypto currencies are backed by faith in their developers. What could go wrong?"[174] This was a surprising analysis from the normally pro-market *Journal* editorial board. For one, while it's largely true that the dollar is the best of an unstable monetary lot, it's surely not lost on the *Journal's* editorialists that the dollar has given its holders at times a wild ride since it was floated in the early 1970s. Put another way, the "government" backing the dollar hasn't always pursued policies rooted in stability or preservation of worker wealth.

This brings us to China in 80 B.C. Since money is as old as commerce, debates about money are similarly old. Notable about China long ago is that there are records of contentious arguments regarding whether currency should be a responsibility of the state or the private sector. According to Eswar Prasad in *Gaining Currency*, "Many Confucian scholars at the time held that a state monopoly on the coinage of money was best avoided as it would allow the state to debase its own coin with impunity. As proponents of reduced state intervention in every aspect of the economy, they made the case that the market would compel private issuers of money to maintain its value."[175] Precisely! Common sense circulated, perhaps more widely, in the B.C. era. Of course, private issuers of money would be more likely to maintain the value of money issued simply because this is what markets demand. What's not monopoly issued must not rip off its customers unless it doesn't mind not having customers. And to be clear, markets demand reasonable money even in times when always-devaluing governments are the monopoly issuer. Stop and think about that for a second.

Consider yet again how the dollar most prominently, but also the euro, Swiss franc, Japanese yen, British pound, Chinese renminbi, and very few other currencies referee serious exchange both globally, but also locally. It's a reminder that just because governments have so much control over the monetary units in 2022 doesn't mean there's not a market for money. Ultimately market actors moving real resources decide what is and is not money. In short, amid a lot of execrable currency options, markets have happened upon the good ones—or the reasonably good ones. Still, we can do better. The speculation here is that the future of private money will have an Amazon quality to it, perhaps Walmart too, or maybe J.P. Morgan. With the mention of these three, ask yourself a question: would you prefer to earn Amazon, Walmart, and J.P. Morgan dollars over the U.S. dollar? The bet here is that more than a few of us would take the private money. Why not? None of the companies mentioned could ever devalue on us. The brand risk is too great, as is the threat of losing hard-won customers. Yet the U.S. Treasury has never been nearly as trustworthy; monopoly issuers don't need to be.

Some are now wondering how this will work, and it's really not terribly complicated. At present we ask business proprietors "Do you take American Express?" or Visa, or Discover, or name your card. Why would cash be any different? Gradually the circulation of good, stable money would grow and grow, and do so naturally. Again, let's never forget that money is a natural consequence of production and exchange; good money naturally pushes out the bad. Why? Once again, none of us want to be ripped off. Which leads to one additional speculation: Elon Musk. It's always struck yours truly as wildly fanciful the presumption that Musk is interested in owning Twitter in order to give various ideologies a place to express their views (as of this writing the buyout's conclusion is uncertain). No doubt that's an intent, but the prediction here is that Musk remains interested in completing the job of revolutionizing finance and money that began at X.com (later PayPal), but that never reached the Musk-ian conclusion of a financial supermarket that would render today's banks and investment banks yesterday's news. The bet here is that a Musk-owned Twitter (or a future Musk startup) will similarly pursue private money, and it will be the right private money. You see, Musk gets it. Return to the quote that begins this chapter. In properly viewing money as an "information system" Musk plainly sees the immense worth of money that has constant qualities as a measure of value.

Of course, whether it's Musk, Twitter, Amazon, Walmart, J.P. Morgan, or not, the end result of businesses issuing trusted private money is not really the point. The point is that a private sector that can erect mile-high buildings and manufacture pocket-sized supercomputers can design money that will push out government pretenders in between breakfast and lunch. Equally critical is that the private sector must do this so that humans with limitless potential can realize a great deal more of it. And so, it will happen.

The future is blindingly bright.

ENDNOTES

1   Jen Wieczner, "Mike Novogratz Talks About His Big Crypto Error," *New York Magazine*, June 27, 2022

2   Annie Roth, "Love Triangle Challenges Reign of Japan's Monkey Queen," *New York Times*, January 21, 2022

3   Ibid.

4   Stefan Al, *Supertall: How the World's Tallest Buildings Are Reshaping Our Cities and Our Lives*, W.W. Norton & Company, 2022, p. 36

5   Matthew Hennessey, Visible Hand: A Wealth of Notions On the Miracle of the Market, Encounter, 2022, p. 9

6   Stefan Al, *Supertall: How the World's Tallest Buildings Are Reshaping Our Cities and Our Lives*, W.W. Norton & Company, 2022, p. 41

7   Ibid, p. 66

8   Ibid, p. 27

9   Ibid, p. 5

10 Ibid, p. 38

11 Ibid, p. 40

12 Leon Walras, *Elements of Pure Economics*, Augustus M. Kelley Publishers, 1977, p. 83

13 David Asman, "The Mobile Guide: Artistes and Apparatchiks," *Wall Street Journal*, August 12, 1992

14 Christopher Leonard, *The Lords of Easy Money*, Simon & Schuster, 2022, p. 111

15 Enrico Moretti, *The New Geography of Jobs*, Houghton Mifflin Harcourt, 2012, p. 10

16 Jennifer Shahade, "How to Accept a Loss," *Wall Street Journal*, June 4-5, 2022

17 Harald Jahner, *Aftermath: Life In the Fallout of the Third Reich, 1945-1955*, Alfred A. Knopf, 2021, p. 13

18 Ibid, p. 166

19 Ibid, p. 187

20 Ibid, p. 180

21 Ibid, p. 191

22 John Maynard Keynes, *A Tract On Monetary Reform*, Prometheus Books, 2000, p. 1

23 Giles Milton, *Checkmate In Berlin: The Cold War Showdown That Shaped the Modern World*, Henry Holt and Company, 2021, p. 103

24 Ibid, p. 106

25 John Stuart Mill, *Principles of Political Economy*, Prometheus Books, 2004, p. 459

26 Craig Karmin, *Biography of the Dollar*, Crown Business, 2008, p. 40

27 George Gilder, *The Scandal of Money*, Regery Publishing, 2016, p. 17

28 Craig Karmin, *Biography of the Dollar*, Crown Business, 2008, p. 19

29 George Gilder, *The Scandal of Money*, Regery Publishing, 2016, p. 44

30 Christopher Leonard, *The Lords of Easy Money*, Simon & Schuster, 2022, p. 96

31 George Gilder, "A 21st Century Case for Gold," American Principles Project, 2015

32 Jimmy Soni, *The Founders: The Story of PayPal and the Entrepreneurs Who Shaped Silicon Valley*, Simon & Schuster, 2022, p. 104

33 Ashlee Vance, *Elon Musk: Tesla, SpaceX, and the Quest For a Fantastic Future*, Ecco, 2015, p. 81

34 Jimmy Soni, *The Founders: The Story of PayPal and the Entrepreneurs Who Shaped Silicon Valley*, Simon & Schuster, 2022, p. 37

35 Ibid, p. xvi

36 Ibid. p. 80

37 Ibid. p. xx

38 Ibid, p. xvi

39 Ibid, p. 170

40 Stephen A. Schwarzman, *What It Takes: Lessons In the Pursuit of Excellence*, Avid Reader Press, 2019, 204-205

41 Jimmy Soni, *The Founders: The Story of PayPal and the Entrepreneurs Who Shaped Silicon Valley*, Simon & Schuster, 2022, p. 317

42 Ibid, p. 329

43 John Stuart Mill, *Principles of Political Economy*, Prometheus Books, 2004, p. 464

44 Jing Yang & Julie Steinberg, "How a 'Surefire' Bet On Ant Group Has Trapped Global Investors," *Wall Street Journal*, February 9, 2021

45 Sebastian Mallaby, *The Power Law: Venture Capital and the Making of the New Future*, Penguin Press, 2022, p. 231-32

46 Ibid, p. 233

47 Ibid, p. 224

48 Sebastian Mallaby, *The Power Law: Venture Capital and the Making of the New Future*, Penguin Press, 2022, p. 42

49 Ibid, p. 89

50 Ibid, p. 145

51 Christopher Leonard, *The Lords of Easy Money*, Simon & Schuster, 2022, p. 7

52 Jeffrey Snider, "Let's Get Ready to Clean Up More of Powell and Yellen's Mess," *RealClearMarkets*, May 27, 2022

53 Christopher Leonard, *The Lords of Easy Money*, Simon & Schuster, 2022, p. 6

54 Adam Liptak & Kevin Draper, "Supreme Court Ruling Favors Sports Betting," *New York Times*, May 14, 2018

55 Allison Prang, "Drug-Smuggling Tunnel Found Linking San Diego to Mexico," Wall Street Journal, May 18, 2022

56 Robert H. Smith, *The Changed Face of Banking*, CreateSpace Independent Publishing, 2014, p. 4

57 Frank Pallotta, "The Huge 'Animal House' Blunder That Cost Donald Sutherland Millions," *Business Insider*, April 3, 201

58 Chris Nashawaty, *Caddyshack: The Making Of a Hollywood Cinderella Story*, Flatiron Books, 2018, p. 82-83

59 Ibid, p. 85

60 Ibid, p. 90

61 Ibid, p. 91

62 Ibid, p.91

63   Ibid, p. 95

64   Andy Kessler, "Hollywood Hates Silicon Valley," *Wall Street Journal*, April 25, 2022

65   Andy Kessler, "Trump Could Be the First Silicon Valley President," *Wall Street Journal*, February 3, 2017

66   Peter Thiel & Blake Masters, *Zero to One*, Crown Business, 2014, p. 84

67   Sebastian Mallaby, *The Power Law: Venture Capital and the Making of the New Future*, Penguin Press, 2022, p. 79

68   Ibid, p. 8

69   Sebastian Mallaby, *The Power Law: Venture Capital and the Making of the New Future*, Penguin Press, 2022, p. 82

70   Ibid, p. 90

71   Ibid, p. 114

72   Ibid, p. 183

73   Ibid, p. 231

74   Ibid, p. 198

75   Ibid, p. 352

76   Christopher Leonard, *The Lords of Easy Money*, Simon & Schuster, 2022, p. 130-31

77   Sebastian Mallaby, *The Power Law: Venture Capital and the Making of the New Future*, Penguin Press, 2022, p. 17-18

78   Christopher Leonard, *The Lords of Easy Money*, Simon & Schuster, 2022, p. 131

79   Eswar Prasad, *Gaining Currency: The Rise of the Renminbi*, Oxford University Press, 2017, p. 10

80   Jonathan Kaufman, *The Last Kings of Shanghai: The Rival Jewish Dynasties That Helped Create Modern China*, Viking, 2020, p. 4

81   Ibid, p. 27

82   Ibid, p. 32-33

83   Ibid, p. 52-53

84   Ibid, p. 117

85 Ibid, p. 84

86 Ibid, p. 149

87 Ibid, p. 162

88 Ibid, p. xxvi

89 Ibid, p. 143

90 Ibid, p. 218

91 Ibid, p. 178-79

92 Ibid, p. 206

93 Ibid, p. 234

94 Ibid, p. xxix

95 Jeanna Smialek, "The Dark Side of the White-Hot Labor Market," New York Times, June 7, 2022

96 Sebastian Mallaby, *The Power Law: Venture Capital and the Making of the New Future*, Penguin Press, 2022, p. 13

97 Ibid, p. 391

98 Ibid, p. 148

99 Ibid, p. 155

100 Ibid, 273-276

101 Heather Somerville, "For Tech Startups, the Party's Over," *Wall Street Journal*, May 16, 2022

102 Nathan Lewis, *The Magic Formula: The Timeless Secret To Economic Health and Prosperity*, Canyon Maple Publishing, 2019, p. 102

103 Steve Forbes, Nathan Lewis, and Elizabeth Ames, *Inflation: What It Is, Why It's Bad, and How To Fix It*, Encounter Books, 2022, p. 18

104 John Maynard Keynes, *A Tract On Monetary Reform*, Prometheus Books, 2000, p. 46

105 Adam Fergusson, When Money Dies, PublicAffairs, 2010 edition, p. 117

106 Christopher Leonard, *The Lords of Easy Money*, Simon & Schuster, 2022, p. 6

107 David Ricardo, *Principles of Political Economy and Taxation*, Prometheus Books, 1996, p. 59

108 Brian Domitrovic, *The Emergence of Arthur Laffer*, Palgrave MacMillan, 2021, p. 48

109 Adam Fergusson, *When Money Dies*, PublicAffairs, 2010 edition, p. 9

110 Ibid, p. 84

111 Ibid, p. 164

112 Ibid, p. 140

113 Jonathan Kaufman, *The Last Kings of Shanghai: The Rival Jewish Dynasties That Helped Create Modern China*, Viking, 2020, p. 206

114 Virginia Lopez Glass, "Virginia's New Lettuce-Based Economy Is Good Enough for Now," New York Times, September 6, 2021

115 Farnaz Fassihi, "With Inflation Ravaging Currency, Iran Is Replacing Names and Numbers," *New York Times*, May 4, 2020

116 Anna Fifield, *The Great Successor: The Divinely Perfect Destiny of Brilliant Comrade Kim Jong Un*, PublicAffairs, 2019, p. 148

117 Stu Woo & Thomas Grove, "Nervous Expatriates Quietly Leave Russia," *Wall Street Journal*, March 9, 2022

118 Anton Troianovski & Patrick Kingsley, "Russians Who Want to Be Anywhere but Russia," *New York Times*, March 14, 2022

119 Eswar Prasad, *Gaining Currency: The Rise of the Renminbi*, Oxford University Press, 2017, p. 110

120 Nigel Lawson, *The View From No. 11: Memoirs of a Tory Radical*, Bantam Press, 1992, p. 783

121 Adam Fergusson, *When Money Dies*, PublicAffairs, 2010 edition, p. 117

122 Steve Forbes, Nathan Lewis, and Elizabeth Ames, *Inflation: What It Is, Why It's Bad, and How To Fix It*, Encounter Books, 2022, p. 23

123 Sebastian Mallaby, *The Power Law: Venture Capital and the Making of the New Future*, Penguin Press, 2022, p. 150

124 Douglas Belkin, "For Top Students, Rejections Pile Up," *Wall Street Journal*, April 22, 2022

125 Eswar Prasad, *Gaining Currency*, Oxford University Press, 2017, p. 187

126 Michael Breen, *The New Koreans: The Story of a Nation*, Thomas Dunne Books, 2017, p. 112

127 Editorial, "The Biden Plan to Raise College Tuition," *Wall Street Journal*, March 30, 2022

128 John Stuart Mill, *Principles of Political Economy*, Prometheus Books, 2004, p. 494

129 Phil Gramm & Mike Solon, "The Democrats' Inflation Blame Game," *Wall Street Journal*, January 13, 2022

130 Carmen M. Reinhart & Kenneth S. Rogoff, This Time Is Different: Eight Centuries of Financial Folly, Princeton University Press, 2009, p. 22

131 Dylan Matthews, "Modern Monetary Theory, explained," *Vox.com*, April 16, 2019

132 Lawrence Goodman, "How the Fed Rigs the Bond Market," *Wall Street Journal*, November 17, 2021

133 Jörg Guido Hülsmann, "The Cultural and Political Consequences of Fiat Money," Mises Institute, November 20, 2014, https://mises.org/library/cultural-and-political-consequences-fiat-money-0. Accessed July 14, 2022.

134 Eswar Prasad, *Gaining Currency: The Rise of the Renminbi*, Oxford University Press, 2017, p. 110

135 Robert L. Bartley, *The Seven Fat Years: And How To Do It Again*, The Free Press, 1992, p. 36

136 Abdi Latif Dahit, "135 Million Face Starvation. That Could Double," *New York Times*, April 23, 2020

137 Lawrence Summers, "The Biden stimulus is admirably ambitious. But it brings some big risks, too." *Washington Post*, February 4, 2021

138 Dan Thornton, "Where Should the Blame Lie for U.S. Inflation?" *Wall Street Journal*, December 19, 2021

139 Judy Shelton, "Fed Interest Hikes May End Up Having Unintended Consequences," *Wall Street Journal*, June 16, 2022

140 John Greenwood & Steve Hanke, "The Fed Needs to Put Its Eye on the Money Supply," *Wall Street Journal*, March 11, 2022

141 John Greenwood & Steve Hanke, "The Altimeter for Powell's Soft Landing," *Wall Street Journal*, April 10, 2022

142 Brian Domitrovic, *The Emergence of Arthur Laffer*, Palgrave Macmillan, 2021, p. 5

143 Holman Jenkins, "Inflation and the Trump Factor," *Wall Street Journal*, June 15, 2022

144 Editorial, "The Fed and Recession Fears," *Wall Street Journal*, June 15, 2022

145 Robert L. Bartley, *The Seven Fat Years: And How To Do It Again*, The Free Press, 1992, p. 51

146 Robert L. Bartley, *The Seven Fat Years: And How To Do It Again*, The Free Press, 1992, p. 52

147 Ibid, p. 109

148 William Greider, *Secrets of the Temple: How the Federal Reserve Runs the Country*, Simon and Schuster, 1987, p. 543

149 Ibid, p. 570

150 Eswar Prasad, *The Future of Money*, The Belknap Press of Harvard University Press, 2021, p. 29

151 Rachel Wolfe, "Teen Babysitters Are Charging $30 an Hour Now, Because They Can," *Wall Street Journal*, May 19, 2022

152 Erich Schwartzel, "Plot Twist! Movie Theaters Fear Popcorn Shortfall Will Be a Spoiler," *Wall Street Journal*, June 1, 2022

153 *Forbes*, "Nokia: One Billion Customers – Can Anyone Catch the Cell Phone King?", February 2007

154 Tunku Varadarajan, "An Insider Explains the Supply-Chain Crisis," *Wall Street Journal*, December 18-19, 2021

155 Kevin Warsh, "The Fed Is the Main Inflation Culprit," *Wall Street Journal*, December 13, 2022

156 David Yaffe-Bellany, "Gas Prices In U.S. Pass $4 a Gallon," *New York Times*, March 7, 2022

157 Gregory Zuckerman, *The Frackers*, Portfolio Penguin, 2013, p. 126

158 Ibid, p. 310

159 Quin Hillyer, "Catch a Falling Dollar!" *The American Spectator*, November 27, 2007

160 Jimmy Soni, *The Founders: The Story of PayPal and the Entrepreneurs Who Shaped Silicon Valley*, Simon and Schuster, 2022, p. 313

161 Carmen M. Reinhart & Kenneth S. Rogoff, This Time Is Different: Eight Centuries of Financial Folly, Princeton University Press, 2009, p. 44

162 Amity Shlaes, *The Forgotten Man: A New History of the Great Depression*, HarperCollins, 2007, p. 148

163 Eric Rauchway, *The Money Makers*, Basic Books, 2015, p. 74-75

164 Amity Shlaes, *The Forgotten Man: A New History of the Great Depression*, HarperCollins, 2007, p. 147

165 Steven F. Hayward, *The Age of Reagan: The Fall of the Old Liberal Order, 1964-1980*, Prima Publishing, 2001, p. 262-63

166 Allen J. Matusow, *Nixon's Economy: Booms, Busts, Dollars, and Votes*, University Press of Kansas, 1998, p. 153

167 Robert H. Ferrell, *Inside the Nixon Administration: The Secret Diary of Arthur Burns, 1969-1974*, University Press of Kansas, 2010, p. 39

168 Eswar Prasad, *The Future of Money*, The Belknap Press of Harvard University Press, 2021, p. 61

169 Corrie Driebusch & Paul Vigna, "The Crypto Party Is Over," *Wall Street Journal*, June 18-19, 2022

170 John Tamny, "We'll Know Crypto Is For Real When Its Coins Start Collapsing," *Forbes.com*, June 6, 2021

171 Steven F. Hayward, *The Age of Reagan: The Fall of the Old Liberal Order, 1964-1980*, Prima Publishing, 2001, p. 7

172 Stefan Al, *Supertall: How the World's Tallest Buildings Are Reshaping Our Cities and Our Lives*, W.W. Norton & Company, 2022, p. 3

173 Brian Domitrovic, *The Emergence of Arthur Laffer*, Palgrave Macmillan, 2021, p. 5

174 Editorial, "Warnings From the Crypto Crash," *Wall Street Journal*, May 13, 2022

175 Eswar Prasad, *Gaining Currency*, Oxford University Press, 2017, p. 4

INDEX

CPSIA information can be obtained
at www.ICGtesting.com
Printed in the USA
LVHW111607221022
731328LV00017BA/662/J